BEYOND TALENT

A Handbook for Performers

Andrea Uselman

Published by Polar Bear

Cover Photography
Phil Leisenheimer
LA Studio
7625 Golden Triangle Drive, Suite J
Eden Prairie, MN 55344

Cover Design
EJ McNulty

ISBN-13: 978-0-578-00328-3

Printed in the United States of America

CONTENTS

From The Author

How This Handbook Can Help You

Overall Approach

Being Your Own Business Partner 7
Staying Informed 7

PART I AUDITIONING

Knowing Your Type 9
Headshots 9
Resumes 11
Resume Example 13
Finding Auditions 14
Making Appointments 15
Preparing for Auditions 16
Character Development 19
Controversial Questions 19
Dress & Appearance 20
Going to Auditions 21
Audition Bag Checklist 22
Audition Jitters 23
Your Audition 25
Movement Auditions 29
Cold Readings 30
Call-Backs 31
Dealing with Rejection 33

PART II THE CREATIVE PROCESS

Stages of the Creative Process 36
Preparation 36
Rehearsal 38
Character Behavior & Development 39
Performance 41
Finding Your Inner Creativity 41

PART III PERFORMER MAINTENANCE

Mental Health & Attitude 44
Vocal & Physical Health 48
Daily Training 50
Vocal Warm-Ups 52
Finding Range & Key Signature 58
Circle of Fifths Chart 59
Physical Warm-Ups 60
Unions 61
Agents, Managers, Casting Directors 63
Networking 65
The Day Job 66
Taxes 67

Final Thoughts

Appendix
Additional Resources 72
Suggested Readings 74

Works Cited

About The Author

FROM THE AUTHOR

As performers, we strive to be great communicators with our audiences; however, it is also essential that we communicate with each other about our craft. We should not view what we do as a mysterious phenomenon, but realize there are ways to steer our paths, take control, and use our talents to our advantage. Learning about music, theatre, dance, and the performing arts business is a great way to ensure you are not only a well-rounded performer, but an informed one.

I wrote this handbook for performers who have an interest in any combination of music, theatre, and dance, and have the desire to make a career out of it. Understanding that technique and talent are crucial elements for pursuing a performance career, this book focuses on what else you will need.

HOW THIS HANDBOOK CAN HELP YOU

Whether you consider yourself a singer, actor, or dancer, this handbook provides practical information all performers can use. It provides helpful tips that aim to fill in the blanks and answer those questions you've wanted to ask.

Being able to compete for work as a "triple threat," someone who is good at singing, acting, and dancing, is a demanding goal. But as many of my professors told me, "the more tools you have in your toolbox, the better." Therefore, this handbook will help you prepare for any audition.

We all know that there is more than one way to do something, which is why I suggest this be a jumping off point for your own research. To provide a wide range of opinions and advice, I have included quotes from students and experienced professionals whom I surveyed while studying at the University of Minnesota. While only you will be able to decide what is right for your personal journey, my hope is that you will feel more confident having this handbook to refer to.

The *Contents* page lists the topics included in the handbook which are organized in three parts: *Auditioning* focuses on what you need in order to get cast, while *The Creative Process* focuses on what happens after you are cast. *Performer Maintenance* has information helpful for sustaining a career in performance, and is followed by resources for further research and a suggested reading list.

OVERALL APPROACH

Being Your Own Business Partner

Choosing to pursue performance is choosing to invest a lot of time in yourself. Let's face it, it requires being your own toolbox and instrument. This means taking care of yourself and constantly reinventing who you are. This does not mean leaving behind your values and personal beliefs. It means being able to market yourself, take rejection, and accept who you are, and where you are in your personal journey. This is even truer if you want to pursue performance as a career.

Having a positive attitude and knowing what your strengths and weaknesses are is important. Taking classes and workshops, and working on techniques are great ways to keep improving yourself. If performing is your passion, don't be overly concerned with what people say. Stay away from negative people in general. Realize that reviews and critics are not the end all, and that whether they have something nice or bad to say, it is only an opinion. Ultimately, all that matters is what *you* think.

On the other hand, never think you know it all or that anyone else knows it all either. Very few people will say that they are not bothered by a person who thinks too highly of themselves or complains too much. Be respectful of yourself and others so that people will want to work with you. This way you will build a good reputation. It will also help you get future roles more than talent or technique in a lot of cases.

Staying Informed

One of the first pieces of advice I got when I started expressing an interest in a performance career was to read anything and everything I can lay my hands on. Staying informed about what is going on in the area is a great way to know what opportunities are available. Reading newspapers, getting news online, and reading fliers and bulletins posted around town are all great ways to stay informed. See shows whenever possible and get familiar with local artists and directors.

PART I: AUDITIONING

In a performing arts career, auditioning cannot be avoided. By being well prepared and informed, you can learn to enjoy the process and avoid unnecessary frustration and stress. Auditioning is a skill that requires constant practice, and like performing, it demands you to be in the moment at all times.

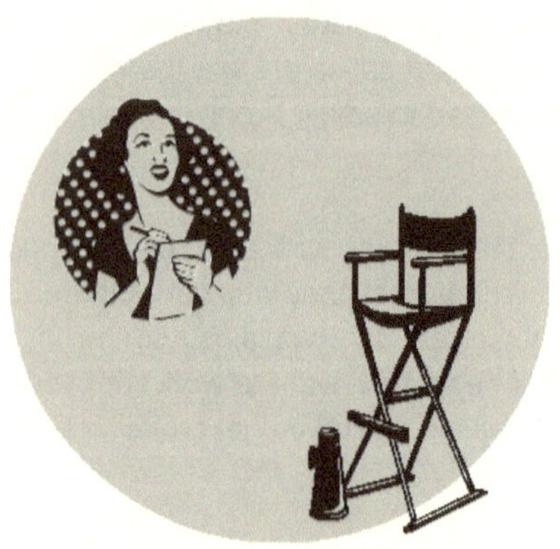

Knowing Your Type

Because there are so many people out there who you will be competing against, it is important to know your type and what kind of performer you want to be. Finding a specific look and knowing what kind of characters you can play will help determine your type and how you market yourself. Although we all want to say we can play a variety of roles, finding specific strengths and focusing on unique characteristics is key to getting a foot in the door.

In Robert Cohen's *Acting Professionally*, he describes the various types of actors as: Children and Preteens, Ingénues (young women) and Young Leading Men (the innocent love interest), Leading Men and Leading Women (the more experienced lover), and Character Men and Character Women (the comedic character or villain). [1]

It is also important to eventually be able to rate which of the three disciplines is your strongest asset, and to know whether you are a Singer/Actor/Dancer, or an Actor/Dancer/Singer, et cetera. It may change over time, but some directors will ask you to label yourself this way. While many people like to simply say "I'm a performer," it is a good idea to keep trying to improve your weaker areas so that you will eventually be strong in all three, hence the term a "triple threat."

Headshots

Having a great photograph is essential. Headshots are intended to catch the director's attention and to help them remember your face. Usually, they are 8x10 inches and are black and white. Although, color is being used currently for commercial and print work. Some people get photos that show 3/4 of their body, but many only show from the chest upward.

Once you have chosen a specific look that fits your type, you are ready to get headshots. Ranging from $200-$500, think of your headshots as an investment in your career and remember if your look changes you'll have to get them retaken. Shop around and ask people who they recommend. Ask to look at samples of their work ahead of time. It is very important to feel comfortable with the photographer to get that perfect shot.

Once you have found a photographer, they will take multiple pictures and will give you what are called composites or contact sheets. These show all the shots you can choose from. Consider having a theatre and commercial headshot so that you have a couple of options. Ask if any prints are included in the fee. Most photographers keep the negatives on file in case you want to get a different picture printed up. In all cases, you will take either an actual print or the negatives to a print shop to get your official copies. Many places offer a student discount if you show your student ID.

Ask friends and family which photos they think best reflect you. Ask your photographer as well. Call up agencies and ask for an agent to take a minute and give their recommendation. Whatever you choose, make sure it's eye catching and reflects your unique personality.

"A picture that is friendly but natural lets me use my "casting imagination" better than a glamour shot."

Barbara Kingsley
Adjunct Faculty
U of MN Department of Theatre Arts & Dance

Headshot Tips

Headshot Tips
Pick a hairstyle that is your current look and is a style that you can wear for all of your auditions.
Keep your hair color fairly natural.
Get your hair cut or colored at least a week before your headshots are taken. This will give it time to relax, and you time in case you need to get an emergency fix.
Men should be freshly shaved.
Wear something classic, and not too trendy.
Dark colors work best, such as black, navy blue, red, and grey.
Keep patterns to a minimum.
Texture is good, such as velvet, corduroy, or sweater material.
Open necklines are good, scooped or V-neck. For men, wearing a dark V-neck layered over something lighter is a great option.
DON'T wear jewelry, it distracts and can date your picture.
Men and Women should wear makeup. Ask your photographer if they can hire a makeup or hair artist for you, or bring your own. Make sure they have done makeup for headshots before.
Bring your favorite music to your photo shoot to help you feel comfortable.
Most importantly, smile and open your eyes wide. Be yourself and exude energy!

"In a "cattle call" of 300-500 people, it is necessary that the picture looks as you do right now and "pops" out when compared to other pictures."

Linda Talcott Lee
Adjunct Faculty
U of MN Dance Program (Jazz and Musical Theatre)

Resumes

Your resume is the way that directors who don't know you can find out your credentials. It documents your personal performance history and should be constantly updated. It also contains your contact information, which is essential if you hope to get a call-back after an audition.

Use a two, three, or four column format. List the show first, followed by your role, the director/choreographer or producer, and lastly, where it took place. Be careful *not* to put things like "The Rarig Center" for University Theatre. Many people have not heard of theater buildings at universities. In this case, it would be best to simply say "University of Minnesota."

Format your resume differently for different auditions depending on the type of show. Have a variety of copies ready if you plan on doing a lot of auditioning. Put the most important things first, depending on what you think the director will want to see. For example, if the audition is for theatre, don't put your film credits first.

If you are just starting out, put down any performance experience you can think of. Try to make it sound special, but don't lie. Definitely list your education and training when you are just starting out, including who you studied with and where. As you gain more experience, list professional work first, followed by community or university theatre experiences, depending on which one you have more experience with. In the beginning, identifying that an experience was professional is fine. Eventually, weed things out as your resume grows and consider removing the title "professional," because any experience is valid whether you are paid or not.

At the bottom, list any special talents or skills you have such as: the ability to speak dialects, to play an instrument, roller skate, do acrobatics, or anything else you feel is special. Make sure you can do what you include. You never know when a director may want to see you do it.

"They provide useful information (*if* they are accurate) However, I would never pre-judge on the basis of resumes... I would need to see and hear the performer."

David Walsh
Director of Opera
U of MN

"Resumes give me an indication of whether the actors have been exposed to a similar working process that I am directing with."

Luverne Seifert
Head of BA Performance
U of MN Department of Theatre Arts & Dance

Resume Tips

Resume Tips
Use double-sided tape, NOT staples, to secure your resume to the back of your headshot.
Resumes will have to be cut to an 8x10 inch size to fit your headshot. Invest in a paper cutter.
Because resumes are often thrown out after auditions, a cell phone number may be better than a home number that is listed next to your address in the phonebook.
DON'T include your address. If you get a call-back or are cast, they will get that information if they want it.
NEVER put your social security number on your resume.
If you have an agent, include their contact information for auditions they set up for you.
Put any union affiliation under your name.
DON'T state your age. You are as old as someone thinks or wants you to be. It is up to you whether you want to put an age range. (People under 18 have to put their age because there are some restrictions.)
Keep it to one page and make sure it is well organized, easy to read, and is not overly crowded. Leave some white space.
DON'T include dates of performances, but reflect your most current work.
Put "Representative of..." before the section with more credits. Pick your best to display. If you have a demo CD, video, or DVD, make sure to list that it is available upon request.
DON'T identify the client or product for commercial work because it cuts you out if a competitor wants to hire you. Include "Commercial Work Available Upon Request" in small print at the bottom of your resume.
Be honest. The director may ask about your past roles or experience working with someone you listed.

"(Resumes) are support materials. If they are professional they add. If poorly done they subtract."

Dawn Baker
Musician/Lecturer
U of MN Department of Theatre Arts & Dance

Resume Example

Your name should be at the top and should stand out.

Include a phone number and an e-mail address. A personal website is a popular and safe way for people to check you out.

Many include height, weight, hair and eye color. If your weight or hair color change, change it on your resume. In some cases, putting height and weight down may limit you. Ultimately, you want to be seen for your talent.

Annie May

Cell 555-555-1234	Height 5'5"	Brown Hair
AnnieMay@theatremail.com	Weight 135	Green Eyes
www.AnnieMay.com		

Theatre Experience

Funny Girl	Ziegfeld Dancer	Rich Raymond	Bloomington Civic Theatre, MN
High School Musical	Gabrielle	Luke Skyler	Children's Theatre Company, MN
The Mikado	YumYum	Amy Teal	G&S Very Light Opera Company, MN
The Rocky Horror Show	Columbia	Melissa Rock	University of Minnesota, Twin Cities
Dracula	Mina Understudy	Kelly Wright	U of MN Centennial Showboat, MN
West Side Story Piece	Somewhere Soloist	Carl Thompson	University Dance Theatre, Twin Cities
The Music Man	Marian	Elizabeth Simon	Lyric Arts Main Street Stage, MN
Anything Goes	Charity	Kelly Booth	University of Minnesota, Twin Cities
Into The Woods	Little Red	Jacob Smith	St. Lawrence Church, MN
The Boyfriend	Maisie	Ashley Hope	University of Wisconsin, Madison
West Side Story	Anybodys	Ben Foss	Stage Works, Stoughton, WI
South Pacific	Nellie	Michael Davidson	Middleton Players Theatre, WI

Education & Training

University of Minnesota, Twin Cities
Bachelor of Arts, Musical Theatre

Opera	Daniel Moore
Voice (Soprano)	Shirley Matthews, Tammy Winter
Acting	Jonathon Michaels
Acting Improvisation	Tom Benson
Auditioning Workshop	Vern Tenor
Voice-Over Workshop	Sam Clipper
Tap	Sarah Gilmore, Kyle Stern
Jazz	Jennifer Peters
Ballet	Emily Brown, Tracey Quinn
Modern	Angela White
African	Roxanne Davis
Musical Theatre	Irma Ryan, Nicole David, Brooke Taylor

Special Skills

Belt Mezzo-Soprano, Basic Piano, Flute, Swing Stunts, Handstand, Whistle, Dialects, Choreography, On Camera, & Print Credits Available Upon Request

Add an "Upon Request" section at the bottom for additional credits to avoid overcrowding.

Finding Auditions

Call Boards

Checking callboards (bulletin boards for posting auditions) is a very common way to find auditions at performing arts schools and universities. Callboards can also be where call-backs and cast lists get posted.

Listserv

Many performing arts organizations and universities have a listserv that you can get e-mails from regarding audition opportunities as well as other theatre news.

School Papers & Newsletters

Smaller university papers and community newsletters can provide specific information related to where you are studying and what is happening in your area.

Student Run Clubs & Organizations

Find out if where you are going to school has any student run groups to get involved with. They are a terrific resource for students to get their questions answered and to get involved.

Classifieds

The classified advertisements in your city paper are often where local auditions are posted. Look under "Performing Arts Careers" in the job section.

Curtain Rising www.curtainrising.com

This is a national website with links to area theaters.

University/Resident Theatre Association (U/RTA) www.urta.com

Each year they audition undergraduate seniors for graduate theatre programs. Students have to be approved by faculty as nominees for what are called the National Unified Auditions, which are held in New York, Chicago, and San Francisco.

Trade Papers

Look for trade papers in your area that have information related to the local music, theatre, and dance scene.

The Back Stage

The *Back Stage* is a newspaper published in New York City for actors, singers, dancers, and the performing community in general. If you want to look at what is going on in the theatre world in New York, check it out. It includes a variety of articles related to Broadway shows, the status of the unions, locations for classes and workshops, available services such as headshot companies, and even information on apartments for performers in New York. It is the primary way to find out about auditions in New York City and the surrounding area. It may also post auditions that are being held in Chicago, Illinois, or dinner theaters like The Fire Side in Fort Atkinson, Wisconsin.

The audition notices in the *Back Stage* are split up into sections such as:
Singers
Theme Parks
General
Dance Stage
Summer Stock
Combined Auditions
Membership Companies
Equity Stage
Chorus Calls
Union/Non-Union Film
Union/Non-Union TV/Video
Non-Union Film
Non-Union TV/Video
Student Film
Late Casting

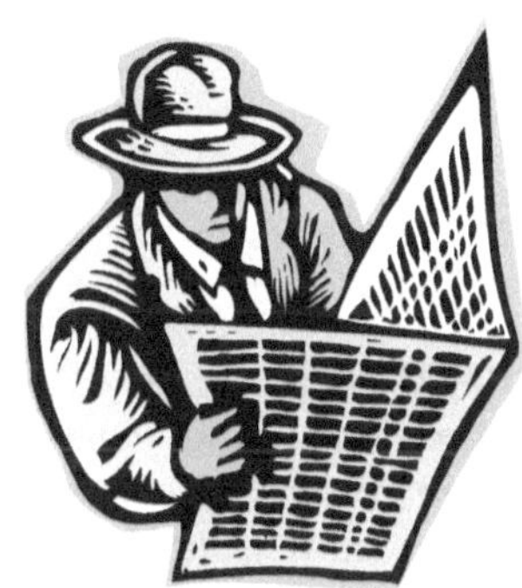

The *Combined Auditions* are those that may involve singing, dancing, and acting, whereas the *Chorus Calls* often specify for "Dancers who sing" or "Singers who move well."

Even if auditioning in New York is an idea down the road for you, reading this trade paper is a great way to keep updated with what is happening in the "Big Leagues." To get a subscription, go to www.backstage.com.

Making Appointments

Once you find an audition you want to go to, you need to either sign your name under a time slot, or call and make an appointment. A sheet is often posted on one of the call boards that you can sign. For any other audition that you find, in the paper or online, you usually need to call and set up a time with the stage manager or person in charge of auditions. Whatever time slot you agree to, make sure it's for a day and time that will work.

If you are calling to set up an appointment, smile when you talk. I once heard that people can tell if you are smiling over the phone, and it can only help. Be friendly, tell the person your first and last name, and that you are interested in making an appointment. They will usually ask if you are Union or Non-Union, which will often determine which time slots they have available for you to audition. After you set up a time, they may tell you what you need to bring or prepare for the audition. If they don't, ask what you will need. Also, ask if there will be an accompanist provided and if you need to dress for movement. Have your questions ready, and get all the information you need. Be professional. Many times, these are the people you will encounter at the audition.

Important Details:

- Date
- Time
- Location
- Requirements
- Call-Back Date

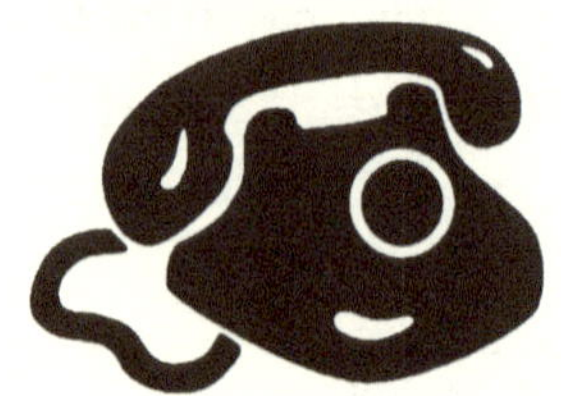

Preparing for Auditions

Do Your Homework

Have at least two contrasting, memorized monologues and songs ready to go at any given moment. You never know when the next audition will come around. Eventually, aim to have around five monologues and as many songs as possible that you can pull out at anytime. The more you have prepared the more options you will have to tailor material to fit specific auditions. Make sure whatever you prepare is appropriate to your age range and type, and really showcases your unique qualities.

Finding good monologues and songs may take some work. Looking through plays and monologue books as well as sheet music at libraries, bookstores, and music shops are great ways to find material. Be careful that a monologue you take from a monologue book is actually from a play. Many directors frown upon ones that are only found in monologue books and nowhere else. If you find a particular musical you want to sing from and have never heard the music before, check out the CD or see if you can listen to it in the store before you buy it. Typically, most people find it harder to find a good monologue than to find a good song.

Look for something that is unique. Try to pick a monologue or song that presents some difficulty, but doesn't stray too far from the mainstream. Look for new playwrights and composers or classic, older standards that most people still appreciate.

Know the Requirements

Number and type of monologues and songs

Usually you will be asked to do 1-2 contrasting monologues and to sing an up-tempo song (peppier, quicker pace) and/or a ballad (slower pace). Monologues can be contemporary, classic, comedic, or have heightened language. Some examples of work with heightened language are by William Shakespeare, Noel Coward, Oscar Wilde, and George Bernard Shaw.

Time constraints

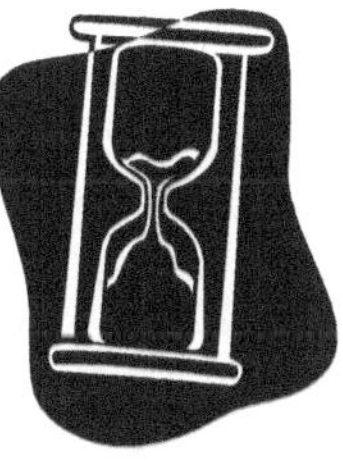

Usually monologues need to be no more than 1-2 minutes in length. Typically, you will be asked to sing a minute or less of a song, which is about 16-32 bars (measures). This may be the refrain of a song. Time how long your monologues and songs are so you know if they will fit within the time constraints of your audition. Respect the time you are allotted, and don't go over. Pace yourself. Nerves will often make you want to go faster.

Whether or not an accompanist will be provided

Bringing your own accompanist is an option, but many times one will be provided. Do not bring a tape or CD to sing along with unless you are specifically asked to.

Whether or not you will be required to do movement

Many times they will not ask you to move unless you get a call-back. If you will be moving, make sure you warm-up prior to going to the audition. Wear warm enough clothes so that you are not cold when it comes time to move.

Research the Show

Find out as much as possible about the production. Research the director and choreographer and know something about the show itself, including the various roles they are auditioning for. Study more than one part, and not only the role you think you would fit the best. You may be asked to read a part you are not expecting.

> ANECDOTE
>
> "Always ask questions about an audition before you get there, or you might find yourself having to jump on a trampoline wearing a swimsuit in front of a room full of people for a summer camp commercial."
>
> **U of MN Senior, Theatre Arts**

Research Your Monologues & Songs

Choose monologues and songs appropriate for the show you are auditioning for. Consider the genre, time period, and type of characters in the show. Usually you do not want to do a monologue or song that is in the actual show. In any case, ask beforehand what they want. Whatever you choose, make sure it shows you at your best.

Know where your monologues and songs come from and what all the words mean. If you are taking a monologue from a scene in a play, read the play in its entirety. Make sure to read the scene you are doing a few times; the same goes for songs. Know something about the shows and characters of the songs you choose. If you are not taking a song directly from a show, know what time period and style it is from and what geographical region it was written in.

Know who the writer and composers are. Be able to pronounce their names correctly. If you do not know, ask someone or look it up.

Prepare & Practice

The more specific you are when developing your monologues and songs the better. Spend time imagining a detailed atmosphere and environment for your character. Imagine yourself in the space you are auditioning in if you know what it will be like. Go over your monologues and songs in front of a mirror, in the shower, and in as many different settings as possible. This will make it easier when the time comes to do them in an unfamiliar setting.

Practice doing your monologues and songs in different circumstances. Practice at different levels of light, volume, and at different speeds of delivery. Ask a friend or two to listen and watch you perform them. Know the material inside and out.

Choose songs that you can perform well and that show your vocal range. Know where your "break" is vocally on the piano (where you have to switch from your head voice to your chest voice). Practice warming up so that you can reach the range you say you are able to sing. Know the range and key signature of your songs. For help on finding the range and key signature, see *Part 3: Performer Maintenance.*

Provide your accompanist with music that is easy to read and in the correct key. Having a three-ring binder works great. Glue or double-side tape each page of sheet music on cardstock (thick paper) and put them in clear, plastic protective pockets in the binder. This allows you the option to pull your song out of the plastic protectors so it can easily be laid out on the piano. Leaving it in the plastic protector can cause glare. Always number your pages so they don't get mixed up. If you have more than four pages, you may want to tape them together in a small chain.

Practice with an accompanist prior to auditioning. Never sing a song at an audition without having heard the piano part. Be comfortable with the speed you like so you can give the accompanist the appropriate tempo. Ask whoever you rehearse with to help you learn the best way to count each particular number you have prepared. Just in case, be able to sing your song a capella (without accompaniment), forwards, backwards, in your sleep, with a different tempo, in a different character voice, et cetera. Be able to hold your own no matter what.

Former University of Minnesota acting professor Kent Stephens has a list of questions to ask yourself when preparing a monologue or song.

Character Development

Who are you?
Who are you talking to? (if it's the audience, what role do they play? Put a name on it...) Who are they to you?
What do you hope to gain from this moment of address- see or hear at the end of it?
What are you trying to keep the listener from getting/finding out?
How does *how* you're saying what you're saying suit your objective? Does it conceal or reveal, act as a vehicle or a smokescreen, et cetera?
What are you *doing*? If there isn't small action, what is your body doing and why?
What are the external distractions, if any?

2

Controversial Questions

Should a person look at the auditors (people listening to you) when auditioning a monologue or song?

- Making eye contact is a very personal thing. Definitely make eye contact when introducing yourself and after you are through.
- Too much eye contact during your performance can be uncomfortable for the people you are auditioning for, because it takes them away from the position of the observer, and includes them in your piece as a participant.
- Most think it is more acceptable for a song, depending on the selection, and think that eyecontact should be made at some point as you sing.
- It is usually best to look just above and past the auditors' heads.
- For both songs and monologues, pretend that you are playing to a full house and include the auditors in that audience.
- Do whatever makes you feel most comfortable. However, if you choose to look at the auditors be prepared for their reaction.

Is auditioning with a monologue you wrote yourself acceptable?

- More people think it is fine to audition with a monologue you write yourself than those who do not think it is a good idea. However, most who say it is fine also say that they know others will disagree.
- If you do write a monologue, make sure it is well written and appropriate for the style of the show you are auditioning for. If you can, ask when you set up the appointment if it would be alright.
- Make sure to test out a self-written monologue before you audition with it, just like you would any other piece.

Is using a prop at an audition acceptable?

- Most agree that props are a huge distraction to an audition and do not recommend using one.
- The only prop that is usually acceptable is a single chair.
- A small prop may be okay if it is used only for manipulation and not aesthetics, and is something a person might normally have, such as tissue, lipstick, or a cell phone.
- Less is more. See if you can get your point across without a prop.

Dress & Appearance

Clothing

Wear clothing that feels good and compliments your particular body type. Ask the opinion of others on your choice of a few outfits specifically picked out for auditions. Have a combination of choices for a variety of auditions. Know what colors you look good in and wear them. Solid colors are easiest to look at. Avoid wild patterns that may distract. If you want to wear black, have a splash of color somewhere for an accent piece so that you can be easily identified.

Make sure the material is not too tight, is free of holes, and is clean and presentable. Women should stay away from shirts that are extremely low cut and skirts that are really short. You want them to want to see more of you, not make them feel like they have seen too much of you. Choosing an outfit that suggests a role is fine, but leave something up to the imagination of the director.

Movement clothing should outline the body, but should never take attention away from you as you are auditioning. Layering helps if you have to do a monologue or song first and want to have your movement clothing underneath.

Undergarments

Wear undergarments appropriate for what you are wearing.
Avoid underwear lines always. Men should bring a dance belt for movement auditions and women should be sure bras are supportive enough for movement. Test out clothing with undergarments before going to an audition. The last thing you want is to feel uncomfortable, or like you have to hold back because you feel awkward in what you are wearing.

Shoes

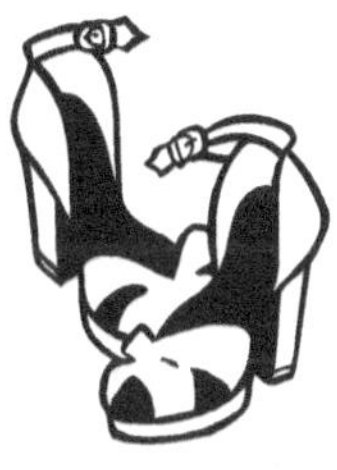

Wear shoes that fit. They should not be too high or noisy, and you should be able to walk easily in them. Steer away from shoes that are too flashy and may be distracting.
Have all the possible shoes you may need for movement with you, and an extra change of socks or tights if you need to change from what you came in.

Hair

Make sure your hair is neat and out of your face. Bring an extra hair tie if you have longer hair and need to pull it back for movement. Wear hair as close to what it looks like in your headshot. Men should shave and be well-groomed.

Makeup

Wear makeup to enhance your look. You want to look your best. Men can even wear a little bit, especially some powder. Don't overdo it, but be confident.

Jewelry

Typically, avoiding jewelry is a good idea. Dangling jewelry is not only distracting but dangerous during movement auditions. Small studs are usually okay, but make sure it is appropriate for the role you are going for. Cover body piercing and tattoos.

Going to Auditions

Practice auditioning. It is an important skill you can develop. The more you do it the better you will get at it, and the better chance you have at getting a part.

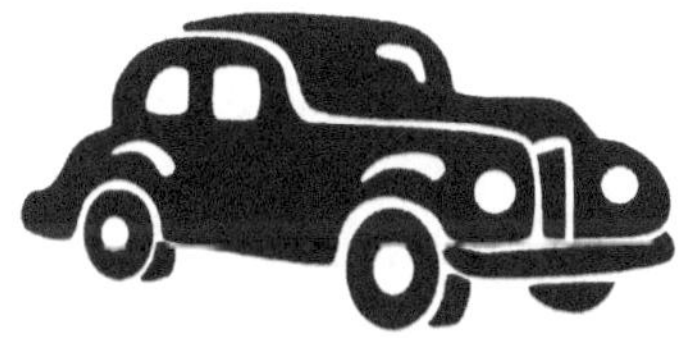

"Audition Buddy"

Is what I like to call a friend who you go to auditions with. They may help you find out about auditions and motivate you to keep auditioning no matter what. I suggest going with someone that is the opposite sex so that you are not in the same category; then you will not have to worry about feeling overly competitive. In the city, it is helpful to have someone to carpool with and find locations for auditions. It is also a nice way to keep your morale up and to look at the experience as an adventure for the both of you. It lessens the stress from only being on you. Although, I suggest this more for people who are new to auditioning. Eventually, going out on your own will probably be more common and convenient. It is still helpful to keep in touch with your fellow performing friends to talk about auditions.

Audition Bag Checklist

Pack your bag the night before to make sure you have everything you need.

Remember to Bring

- ☐ **Directions to Audition**
- ☐ **Resume**
- ☐ **Headshot**
- ☐ **Sheet Music** (Extra options if you are asked for something else)
- ☐ **Clothes for Movement**
- ☐ **Shoes** (Any combination you may need: character shoes, which are heels for women, tap, jazz, or ballet flats)
- ☐ **Tape/Digital Recorder with Headphones** (For learning music fast)
- ☐ **Pitch Pipe** (In case you need to sight sing, which means singing something you have never seen before)
- ☐ **Water Bottle**
- ☐ **Snack** (Apple/Energy Bar)
- ☐ **Calendar** (With your schedule information in case of a call-back)
- ☐ **Anything Else?** (Makeup for touch ups,Hair Ties, Comb, Deodorant)

Arrive Early

Usually 25-30 minutes is sufficient if you have a set time. This allows time to warm-up, touch up hair or makeup, get a drink of water, and get mentally geared up for your audition. It also provides enough time to fill out any information needed from you and to adjust to the space you are in.

If it is an "open-call," such as at some Non-Union auditions where you don't have a set time, get there even earlier if you suspect you may have to wait in line to check-in.

In all cases, drink lots of water beforehand and make sure to warm-up vocally prior to going to the audition. Be careful not to overexert yourself on the day of the audition. Save something. Know your material so well that you do not have to go over it at the audition. Going over the very start and end of each piece can be helpful, but avoid reciting the entire piece right before you have to do it. This prevents a total mind block. Do vocal warm-ups, relaxation, and breathing instead.

Exude Confidence & Be Respectful

The audition starts the moment you walk in the door. First impressions are everything. Be friendly to others auditioning. Smile and make eye contact with the person that you give your information. These individuals often work closely with the director. Avoid wearing perfumes or colognes. Many people are sensitive to smells.

Zoe Sealy, former head of the Jazz Dance Program at the University of Minnesota, suggests turning off your cell phone and pagers, not chewing gum, and never making excuses, such as being injured or having a cold, et cetera. [3]

Audition Jitters

Everyone, no matter how long they have been in the business of performing and auditioning, gets nervous at times. What are known as "butterflies" in the stomach are often a good feeling to have because it gives you energy to put into your work. "Stage fright" on the other hand, is energy put forth to ask yourself "how am I doing?" instead of focusing your energy into your performance. The best way to get rid of these sorts of jitters is to take out the evaluation and get outside of yourself. STOP WORRYING! This may all be easier said than done. Some experience stage fright more than others, but learning a few tricks in how to deal with it can be very helpful. There are three things that I have found work the best.

Relaxation

Take a few minutes to either lie on the floor or sit in a chair with both feet flat on the floor. Let your arms dangle at your sides. Close your eyes and focus on breathing slowly and deeply. Start at the top of your head and work your way down to your feet by telling each area of your body to relax and release tension. Most people carry a lot of tension in their shoulders. It often helps to spend extra time focusing on the areas you hold tension. Once you reach your feet, go back and do a once over to make sure you are relaxed. I notice a huge decrease of nervousness at auditions when I use this relaxation technique.

> "Fear comes when it is about us. Make it be not about you. Fear will stop all progress and ruin your career. Don't be hard on yourself. There are plenty of other people that will do that for you. Many times it's ego."
>
> **Shirley Venard**
> **Teaching Specialist**
> **U of MN Department of Theatre Arts**

Focus on the Task at Hand

After you are relaxed, think about completing the task at hand. At an audition, your goal is to present yourself in the best way you can. Instead of worrying about how you are going to come across, try focusing your attention on the task. Each of your songs and monologues have individual tasks or problems that need to be solved. If you focus on solving the task, you will be less concerned about how you look to others and will have much more success in controlling jitters. Try saying to yourself, "I am here to solve your problem. I am exactly what you need."

Imagine All the Possible Outcomes

One more way to help control your thoughts at an audition is to imagine the various outcomes the audition might have. Close your eyes and imagine seeing all the possibilities, good and bad. Imagine that each are within your reach. Make sure to include something that you might never think will happen. Making it more like a "Choose Your Own Adventure" can make the experience less scary.

> **Putting a touch of lavender aroma therapy scent on your wrists, temples or under your nose can calm nerves..**

"The purpose of an audition is just to show someone else what you already know you can do. It's a sharing of talent."

U of MN Junior, IDIM

"Go in with the intention of entertaining the director, not being judged by them."

U of MN Sophomore, Theatre Arts

"Visualize you already have the part."

U of MN Senior, BA Theatre Performance

"Imagine they are your friends."

U of MN Graduate Student, Vocal Performance

"Breathe- When you perform, don't think about what you're doing, just do it."

U of MN Freshman, Vocal Performance

"Choose specific goals to achieve during an audition."

U of MN DMA first year, Vocal Performance

"I tell myself it's not the end of the world if I don't make it into a piece. It's just another chance to perform and do something you love. I often let myself get too excited when I am about to perform and then I don't breathe and get tired fast, so I usually do a movement and breathing series to make me feel at ease."

U of MN Senior, BFA Dance & BA Theatre Arts

Your Audition

Your Entrance

Walk in with a smile. Say hello and make eye contact with the director, accompanist, and anyone else that is in the room. Give your music to the accompanist and briefly go through it with them, showing any changes or cuts made on the score, and explaining the tempo that you would like. 4

Walk to the center of the space in front of the auditors. Do not stand too close. On more than one occasion, I have been told to stand further back. Most directors want to see you from a bit of a distance to imagine how you may look on stage. Try to make sure you are in the light as well.

Introductions

Introduce yourself clearly, saying your first and last name and what you will be sharing. Say the title of the monologue or song and what show it is from, as well as the playwright or composer. You can introduce more than one monologue at the beginning if you want to immediately transition into another piece. Introduce multiple songs one at a time before performing each piece to give the accompanist a moment to prepare and transition.

ANECDOTE

"When auditioning for *Theatre in the Round,* I was so nervous that I asked where the audience was going to be sitting."

U of MN Senior Theatre Performance

Your Time to Shine

Think of your audition as a performance, and actually *perform* your pieces. Think that you have nothing to lose and that you only live once. Take a good breath, and go for it!

Do the song or monologue that you are most comfortable with first. First impressions are important and it gives you more confidence for your next piece. Sometimes the director may only have you do one of the required monologues or songs if they are pressed for time. Make sure they see what you are the most confident at.

To start your accompanist, make sure they are ready, take a breath, and nod your head. If the tempo gets off, stay strong and hopefully they will follow you. Don't snap your fingers and do not look at the accompanist during the song if things go wrong. Looking at them for help or to fix a tempo only takes away from your performance and breaks your character. [5]

Don't fidget and try to use fewer gestures so that attention is drawn more to your face and voice. Before auditioning, have someone watch or videotape you so you know what your typical mannerisms and tendencies to fidget are.

Don't speed through your pieces. We often want to go faster when we are nervous. Continue to breathe and be aware that you may need to pay extra attention to keep your pace under control.

Transitions

Transitions between monologues and songs should not take too long. A simple change of focus and a breath is sufficient. Between songs, make sure your accompanist is ready. You should not appear to need a lot of preparation and you do not want to go over your time limit.

Your Exit

Once you are done, smile and pause a moment. Never apologize for anything. Maintain eye contact and pay attention to whether the director seems to have any questions for you. If they do, answer honestly and with confidence. Keep in mind that directors want to work with people who want to work with them. If they thank you, smile, and say something like "My pleasure," or how you have enjoyed the experience. Make sure to grab your music and exit with confidence no matter what the experience was like and no matter what their response was.

WHAT THEY LOOK FOR IN AUDITIONERS:

"Technique, charisma and confidence. The first thing I notice is a performer's "look." Are they the right type or adaptable enough to play the part? Do they have the ability to pick up the style and make it believable? Does the performer have a positive, professional attitude?"

Linda Talcott Lee
Adjunct Faculty
U of MN Dance Program (Jazz and Musical Theatre)

"I look for someone who 'pops out' or draws my attention, someone who is charismatic and is a quick study."

Zoe Sealy
Former Head of Jazz Dance Program
U of MN Department of Theatre Arts & Dance

"(An) actor's confidence evident in entrance, posture demeanor, countenance (joyful and enthusiastic), command of the audition material."

Shirley Venard
Teaching Specialist
U of MN Department of Theatre Arts

"Does the person enjoy performing? Do they have histrionic/vocal talent? Do they understand their character and can they render it credibly?"

David Walsh
Director of Opera
U of MN

"I'm pretty open and don't care about presentation until a person performs. However if someone seems to be unprepared or I get any sense they might be difficult to work with that could negate a really good audition."

Joe Chvala
Artistic Director
The Flying Foot Forum

"Most auditions are for a specific role or task. I look for the ability to perform that role or task. I also like to see courtesy and professionalism. If somebody gives off diva-vibes or is unprofessional I probably won't hire them no matter how much ability they have."

Drew Gordon
Musician in Residence
U of MN

"Preparation, being present, being a good type."

John Gamoke
Actor/Affiliate Faculty
U of MN Department of Theatre Arts

"Energy, confidence, attitude, preparation, commitment to the material, passion."

Dawn Baker
Musician/Lecturer
U of MN Department of Theatre Arts & Dance

"Technical proficiency, performance presence (charisma, projection), confidence and ease."

Maria Cheng
Associate Professor
U of MN Department of Theatre Arts & Dance

"Is the auditioner playful, sincere, clear? Is the auditioner open to the world, accepting, generous?"

Luverne Seifert
Head of BA Performance
U of MN Department of Theatre Arts

"Composure, focus, living in the moment as the character."

Barbara Kingsley
Adjunct Faculty
U of MN Department of Theatre Arts

"Vocal quality, diction, deportment."

Elizabeth Nash
Associate Professor
U of MN Department of Theatre Arts & Dance

Movement Auditions

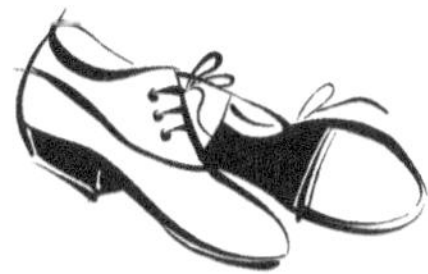

Be focused and pay close attention to what is being asked of you. Ask questions only after you are taught a sequence of movement. "Listen before you ask a question to make sure the question has not already been asked." 6

Try to pick up the movement of the feet first and the rhythm. Add the arms and style of the movement after you have the feet. I find it helpful to not always think of left and right, but to think of upstage (away from the audience) and downstage (towards the audience) when trying to remember which foot to move or which way to face when moving on angles. This also helps if you are asked to reverse something on the spot.

If you get confused, latch on to the feeling or emotion of the piece. Ask if you are unsure what that should be. A choreographer usually loves to talk about that aspect, and would rather not repeat what the steps are. Many times, they will first look at how you can bring a character to the movement, and then they will check to see if you are getting all the moves exactly right.

Make yourself available by standing in front. Mark or go through the movements when you are being taught. Do movements full-out at some point if you can before doing it in a smaller group. If you are at all unsure of a movement when it is time to do it in a smaller group, go for it anyway. Many times a choreographer is also looking for someone who is not afraid to try anything. They will appreciate your positive attitude and full effort. Be confident with yourself and smile. Technique is important, but having stage presence and a unique character is often more eye catching at an audition.

Respect others when they are auditioning. Don't talk or draw attention to yourself in a distracting way. Realize that everyone has different strengths and weaknesses. Don't be intimidated by others. Have the attitude that you have something to offer.

Movement Audition Tips

- DON'T compare yourself to other dancers.
- Remain calm and relaxed.
- DON'T go first or last.
- Breathe and don't freak out.
- Stand at attention.
- Steal style from other people.

ANECDOTE

"When auditioning for the original company of "Beauty and the Beast," I fell flat on my rear end during the dance call. I quickly popped up and fortunately, got a call-back. Trying to make a joke about my temporary clumsiness, I pretended to trip each time I entered the room to sing, read sides, et cetera. I was cast as the "Fainting Silly Girl." To my knowledge, I don't think that character was originally supposed to have that characteristic. Don't be afraid to be yourself and to use your own imperfections for good."

Linda Talcott Lee
Adjunct Faculty
U of MN Dance Program (Jazz and Musical Theatre)

ANECDOTE

"I auditioned for a musical that had a lot of tap dancing in it, but I was not very skilled in that area at all. We auditioned in a carpeted room, so I just plastered on a huge smile and faked my way through the combination. Not only did I get the part, I got picked to do a tap duet. One of my friends was good at tap, so I had him give me lessons and more lessons throughout the course of the show."

U of MN Sophomore, IDIM Music Theatre

Cold Readings

Sometimes you will be asked to read from the script of the show you are auditioning for. Many times you will not be familiar with the script. Ask for the time to look over it before you are asked to read for the director. Many times "sides" or copies of the scene are available ahead of time. You just need to ask the stage manager or person in charge of auditions.

Be flexible and jump right into whatever the director wants you to do.

ANECDOTE

"My first audition at the University I was asked to lie down on the floor and rise up and walk about the room as awaking from a coma. As I prepared to do this, freaked out by how weird it was, the director leaned out and said "Oh, and sing a lullaby." I did the audition and had never felt like a larger moron in my entire life. However, I got in the show and learned a lot. So make every experience count. Throw yourself in the work no matter how weird it seems on the surface."

U of MN Senior, Theatre Arts BA

Cold Reading Tips

Make strong choices that will make you stand out from others.
Make choices that are unpredictable or are the opposite from what most people are likely to do.
Think about the physicality of the person you are being asked to play.
Look up from the script but keep your thumb on the script in one hand so that you don't lose your place.
If you lose your place, don't sweat it, just continue on confidently.
For parts that move fast, keep your eye on the script.
Take your time and be available to whoever you are reading with so that you can react to what they are doing.
If someone that you are reading with has their head in the script and refuses to react to anything you say, move closer to them and try to make eye contact to get them to react to you.
Remember, no matter what you do you will most likely not do exactly what the director is looking for, so make your own choices and be confident with them.

Call-Backs

Wear the same clothing, shoes, hairstyle, et cetera, from your audition to a call-back for easier identification. Many times, people will not remember your name, but will remember how you looked at your audition.

If you are asked to redo your monologue, song, or read the script a second time, do it exactly how you did it the first time. You get a call-back because they like what they saw and you should be able to recreate it.

THE CALL-BACK PROCESS:

"I call back 'potential' then stretch in by asking the performer to make adjustments within a scene or monologue. I am looking to see how directable he or she is. I'll even switch the circumstances to test risk factor."

Barbara Kingsley
Adjunct Faculty
U of MN Department of Theatre Arts

"I will generally have a movement call-back that speaks to the specificity of the show."

Luverne Seifert
Head of BA Performance
U of MN Department of Theatre Arts

"It varies from show to show, but in general songs from the musical are used at call-backs and the director/musical director mixes and matches people they see working together."

Dawn Baker
Musician/Lecturer
U of MN Department of Theatre Arts & Dance

"Call-backs are tough. Usually, for me anyway, call-backs happen when there's a hard decision between two or three folks for one role. You kind of hope the call-back will contain an unexpected event that helps you decide."

Drew Gordon
Musician in Residence
U of MN

"Call-backs are usually about looking for very specific things in a performer, also making sure that my initial impression was right, and pairing people that have a chemistry/look that works together."

Joe Chvala
Artistic Director
The Flying Foot Forum

"I usually make most decisions after the first set of auditions. I only use call-backs if I am very undecided or if someone in whom I am interested was indisposed the first time."

David Walsh
Director of Opera
U of MN

"It depends on the project; however, usually the dance call requires more ability. The readings and vocal call-backs are done so as to target the performer for a particular spot, such as reading sides and singing a song that are done by a specific character."

Linda Talcott Lee
Adjunct Faculty
U of MN Dance Program (Jazz and Musical Theatre)

Dealing with Rejection

The first piece of advice is: get used to it, it's part of the business. The second, try and change your attitude about it. Think about auditioning as your *job*. You have succeeded no matter what the outcome because you simply completed your audition. It is your job to audition, and someone else's job to cast you. *Never* take it personally. There are so many things that go into casting that you will not even be aware of at the time. You may simply have the wrong hair color or be the wrong height next to another person a director wants to cast.

"There are three kinds of performers: #1 Talented Confident, #2 Talented Unconfident, #3 Not Talented Confident. The ones who get hired more often are #3 because they give the director the most opportunity to see them take chances."

Shirley Venard
Teaching Specialist
U of MN Department of Theatre Arts

Audition Journal

Keeping a log of all of the auditions I have gone to in the last five years or so has been extremely helpful. Not only is it a way to keep a list of places and people I have auditioned for, but it is a way to reflect on each particular experience. Rereading entries, I have learned about a few recurring tendencies I have, and can track personal growth.

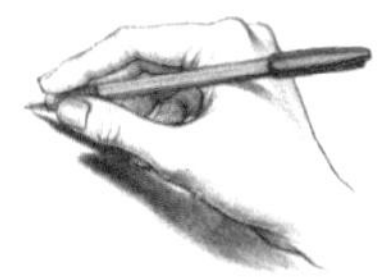

I suggest finding a small notebook especially for audition information. Have space for writing down what you prepared, and how the experience went. Note what clothing you wore in case of a call-back, and later record if you get the part. Sometimes writing funny things that happened and preoccupations you may have had are interesting to note too. All of this may seem arbitrary at the time, but you may find it helpful later when you reread about an experience and look back on other auditions.

For example, there was one audition when I had a cold. I was sitting on the floor touching up my lipstick after I had just blown my nose. I dropped my lipstick, which made a huge red mark on my pants. I was so preoccupied with trying to get myself cleaned up that when I was called in right as this was happening, I had to strongly refocus on doing my best. Despite this chaos, I had one of the best auditions I can remember. Sometimes the things that you think are going to hold you back end up helping you out.

Rejection Tips

Think of the audition as a free class, or a chance to learn something.
Know that other opportunities are just around the corner if it doesn't work out.
Plan something to do after the audition so that it is not the primary focus of the day.
You have not failed if you were prepared and tried your best.
Focus on your personal progress and improvements you've made.
See the show you are not cast in.
DON'T get your hopes up for any part before you get it.
Go into every audition knowing that there are any number of possible outcomes, some within your control and some out of your control.
Let people in your life know that rejection is a part of the business and that they should not feel sorry for you if you don't get a part.
Remember, even people who have been in the business for years have to audition and get rejected.
Look at the humor of any situation and the experience as a whole.
Keep in mind any inspirational words or conversations you've had with people who care about you.

PART 2:
THE CREATIVE PROCESS

If there is one thing I have learned, it is that everyone works differently. Being flexible when working with others is very important. Knowing something about your own creative method and how others work and rehearse is beneficial when adjusting to different creative processes.

The role of the performer is to be available to the director and creative team to help produce a cohesive vision. This means taking direction and being able to adjust to new ideas. It helps to have some ideas about what you would like to do as well. Ultimately, most directors will say they would much rather work with someone who takes direction, than with someone who is close minded and unable to adjust to changes. Remember, it is a constant process, never perfect, and always evolving.

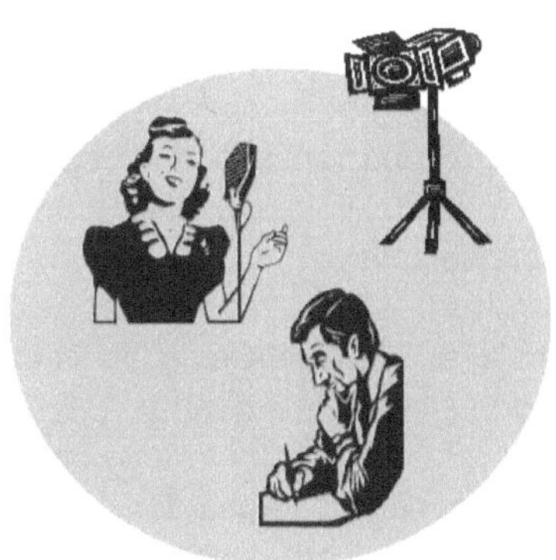

Stages of the Creative Process

Yes, there are stages to developing a character and putting together a production. Understanding these stages can make the experience less overwhelming and more enjoyable. Keeping in mind where you are in the process is key to knowing what to expect and what you will be responsible for. While each individual rehearsal experience and production will be unique, these steps continue to be present in most of them. *Preparation* is gathering facts, ideas, et cetera. *Exploration* is what improvisation is all about: giving up control, experiencing, and exploring options. *Illumination* is the "ah-hah" moment, and creating your choices. *Manifestation* is the result of creative exploration, or when you do the work. [7]

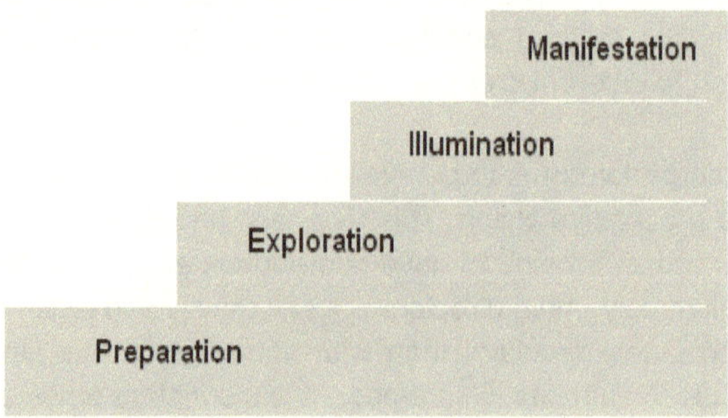

Preparation

If you have got to this point, congratulations! Pass Go and collect $200! You have been cast in a production and can enjoy the beginnings of a new creative process. Being prepared ahead of time makes the rehearsal process and performance go much more smoothly.

Be on time, which means ahead of time. Being late is extremely unacceptable in any rehearsal and performance commitment.

Have all the things you need for rehearsal, including shoes, rehearsal clothes, your script and/or musical score, a pencil, notebook, water, a snack for a break, et cetera.

Wear rehearsal clothes that are similar to your costume so that you will be used to it when the time comes to add costumes. If possible, wear the shoes you will be wearing in the show at rehearsal.

Be ready to work and be attentive. Make sure you have eaten something recently so you have energy.

Turn off your cell phone, and don't wear perfume or large jewelry.

Ask right away when you need to be "off book," or have your lines memorized. Usually at the first rehearsal, sometimes before, you will receive a script and/or musical score. Sometimes it will need to be memorized as early as the first rehearsal if you get the script ahead of time. It has happened to me before. It is your responsibility to know your lines and is unprofessional and a waste of fellow actors' time if you are unprepared at any point in the process. Be prepared and follow the deadlines.

Write down "blocking," or stage directions and movement, and use it to help memorize a scene or song. Use abbreviations such as: cross R/L (Right/Left), or move U/D (Up/Down) to help you write quickly. When you look at the audience from on stage, stage right is to your right, and down stage is toward the audience.

Ask if you can highlight lines in the script or musical score. You may be asked to return it later.

Use sticky tabs for marking each scene you are in, and for marking where songs are interjected. This can help you get an idea of the outline of the show.

Look at the translation or meaning of the text when specifically trying to memorize music. Identify the overall feeling of the song, and then look for contrasts to that feeling in order to add interest.

Always mark with pencil in case you need to make a change.

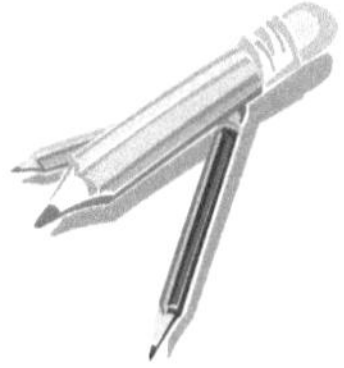

Go over changes before the next rehearsal. It is your job to remember what changes have already been gone through. Keeping a little notebook handy to write down your corrections really helps. If you are unsure about something, ask your director if you can have a few minutes after rehearsal. But by all means, take corrections seriously. No one wants to give or be given the same correction over and over again.

Think about the actions you can play. The more precise you are with identifying shifts and specific actions, the clearer your acting will be. Even if you are asked to do it differently at rehearsal, it is important that you make a choice. But don't get too attached to any one choice of action, in fact, setting one action too early on can set you up for leaving out better options you may discover later.

Think about what words to stress (the operative words). Changing what words are stressed is helpful to keep your delivery fresh, but it can also change the meaning. Use this carefully. Some directors will specify what they want you to stress.

Always check your props before any rehearsal or performance.

Rehearsal

I combine *Exploration* and *Illumination* into one step referred to as *Rehearsal*. Exploration means being flexible and using improvisational skills to explore the options. Illumination means finding out which choices work the best and are what the director wants to see you create.

While taking *Intermediate Acting* at the University of Minnesota, taught by Kent Stephens at the time, we talked a lot about how to develop a character and the differences between preparing and rehearsing a role.

Differences Between Preparation & Rehearsal

"We prepare objectively, we rehearse subjectively. Preparation views a character in the past, present, and future. Rehearsal is only in the moment. Preparation is about differences. Rehearsal is about similarities: the character's goals become your goals, the character's obstacles your obstacles." [8]

Like real life, in acting we put on different masks for different situations. Stephens explains the importance of looking at the behavior of your character both objectively and subjectively.

Character Behavior

Objective	Subjective
What does the character look like to others?	What do you (the character) look like to yourself?
What does the character sound like to others?	Do you like how you sound when you talk?
What small action is the character doing?	What are you avoiding doing or thinking or feeling by doing this?

9

Below are more questions based on "The Ten Big Questions," written by the famous German actress and teacher Uta Hagen. Stephens has revised them slightly.

Character Development

What do you want?
What is your immediate strategy for getting what you want?
What are the immediate external obstacles to getting what you want?
What are the given circumstances? What has brought you to this pass?
What do you want to hear from the other characters that will support or satisfy your objective?
What do you hear in the scene that causes you to change your strategy, if anything?
How does your language suit your objective? Does it state or conceal it, et cetera?
Where and when are you and how does this affect your strategy? What are the environmental distractions, if any?
What are you *doing*? What small action supports your strategy? (Or belies it...)
What *one* answer above can you play when you get on your feet? What *one* answer will get you to what Chaikin calls the One Clear Place? (Or do you need to ask a different question...?)

10

Stephens explains how developing your character transitions into believing whole-heartedly in everything about your character. It is important to eventually leave the intellectual side out of it and to let go.

> "Character Advocacy means not just understanding your character, but loving your character. You cannot hold your focus internally, but should focus outward in pursuit of an objective. "It is always about the other person in acting."
>
> **Kent Stephens**
> **Acting Faculty, Emerson College**

Rehearse like you are in performance.
Don't think waiting until you have an audience will solve all your problems.

Take risks, this is the only way you will be able to test yourself and what you are capable of doing. Your director will love you for it.

Be flexible. Be open to new ideas and willing to try new options.

Be aware of potential problems. Although many unexpected things will happen in performance, costumes will break, trap doors won't open or close, someone will forget a line, rehearsal is the time to try and fix potential problems. Keep in mind your safety and the safety of others. Let your stage manager, director, or choreographer know if you are uncomfortable with anything you are being asked to do. Nothing is worth getting hurt over. If you have a problem with a prop, costume change, or another performer, talk to your stage manager.

Be able to learn and change movement quickly. Choreographers and directors will often change material and you will be required to adjust accordingly.

Respect props and costumes. Many people work very hard on making you look good, which means you need to be careful with what you hold, dance around, or wear on stage. This means putting back all of your props and costumes where you got them from. Never touch another person's prop without permission. If anything is wrong with a prop or costume, let somebody know.

Keep side conversation to a minimum. Time is limited in many rehearsals and your director, choreographer, and fellow actors deserve attention.

Performance

Although most of us enjoy the entire creative process, we usually find performance, or the *manifestation* of all of our hard work, to be the most exciting step. Once you have prepared and rehearsed, it's time to perform in front of an audience.

The desire to give to your audience is something you must have. If you perform only to get applause, you might as well rethink just why you want to be a performer in the first place. Audiences want to see you do well and they want to be moved. It is your job to move them. Any energy you take thinking about yourself when you are performing, and not your character, is energy you take away from what you can give to the audience.

Staying in the moment is key. As my high school theatre director use to tell me, "Acting is reacting. Whatever you hear and say is always happening for the first time." This means being on your toes at all times and always listening. He also said, "The joy is in the performance." It is a joy to perform, and a privilege. Put passion into your character and give all that you can. If you love what you do it won't matter whether you get a standing ovation or not.

Finding Your Inner Creativity

Everyone goes through periods in their life when they have blocks of creativity. It can be for many reasons, but many times it's caused by doing too much of the same thing for too long.

HOW TO KEEP THE CREATIVE JUICES FLOWING:

"Take class to help the mind's quickness on picking up choreography and keep your creativity moving. See as much musical theatre as you can."

Linda Talcott Lee
Adjunct Faculty
U of MN Dance Program (Jazz and Musical Theatre)

"See a variety of theatrical, musical, and arts events. Set up your own performance or improvisation group."

David Walsh
Director of Opera
U of MN

"If no one is hiring you, find yourself a venue, do your own show, do social dance and singing."

Joe Chvala
Artistic Director
The Flying Foot Forum

"Variety is needed to clean the palate. Looking at (or even creating) visual art works great for me in keeping my musical imagination going."

Drew Gordon
Musician in Residence
U of MN

"Keep learning, keep growing, keep studying great performances. Be curious!"

Dawn Baker
Musician/Lecturer
U of MN Department of Theatre Arts & Dance

Free-Writing Journal

Free-writing in a journal is a helpful tool to open up creativity and get your mind flowing. I wrote three pages a day, five times a week, for a semester and found it to be a great tool. At first, it seems like a huge task, but eventually you get better at it. You may find yourself writing about your dreams and ideas about the world. It takes about twenty minutes of your time each day. I liked to do it over my breakfast in the morning, but you can do it before bed as well. If you are having a hard time feeling creative, it helps get your mind to run wild. The object is to put your pen down on the paper and start writing whatever comes to your mind. Don't edit anything or worry about spelling, grammar or if you finish a sentence. Just write. Have a special notebook for your entries, and put it in a secure place. The writing is not meant for other people to read. You do not even have to reread it yourself. A lot of times it will not make sense, like a crazy dream. I even shredded mine after the semester was over for fun. Let me tell you, it is a unique experience. Give it a try.

PART 3: PERFORMER MAINTENANCE

Because you are your biggest asset, it is extremely important to maintain your health, both mentally and physically. There are so many things that are out of your control, so everything you can do to prevent hardship is to your advantage.

In order to sustain a career in performance, you must immerse yourself in the business. You may think about becoming a part of the Actors' Union or one of the many talent agencies. Learning how to network is extremely important, as is finding a good day job and learning how to get the most out of your taxes.

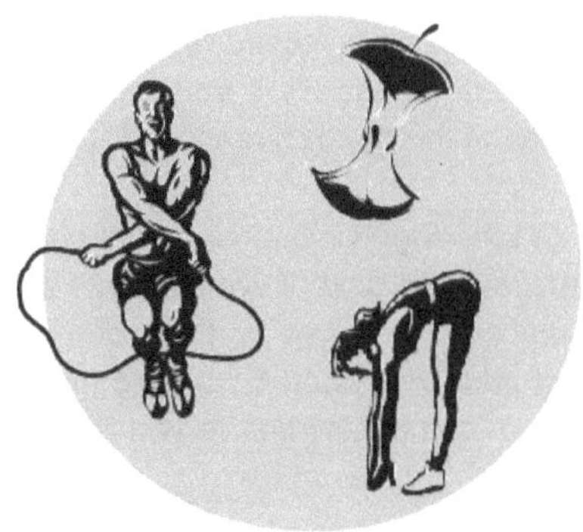

Mental Health & Attitude

Having Dreams & Setting Goals

You have the right and obligation to take control of your life. Having a path and set of goals in mind will help you get what you want out of life. Learning to listen to your inner self and finding what you, not everyone else, want for yourself is very important. Think about where you would like to be two, five, ten years down the road. It will most likely change, but you will have a direction to go toward.

Your goals don't all have to be big. Setting smaller, more attainable goals may help you get to the bigger goals. Whatever the goal, push yourself to use your full potential. Who knows what will come your way?

Be flexible and allow opportunities that come along the way help guide you. Keep your core beliefs and values in mind to avoid regret in the future. Remember, all jobs are learning experiences, but you can choose what you agree to.

Many people think going to New York or Los Angeles is the next step for any recent graduate in the performing arts. This is just not the case. You don't have to "make the move" if you don't want to. In fact, if you don't have a Union Card you probably shouldn't. There is so much more competition today then there was ten, twenty, or fifty years ago. If you lack the credentials of Union Membership and an expansive resume, your options are limited. From what I have been told from those that have moved to New York, waiting until you are thirty to go is not a bad idea, especially if you are female. There just are not that many parts for women in their early twenties. Bottom line, there is no rush.

If moving to New York or Los Angeles is in your immediate future, make sure to have some financial security. The cost of living is quite a bit higher than in most other areas. Visit the place a few times so that you feel comfortable with the surroundings. Keep in contact with people who live in the area so that you will have friends and a sense of community before you move.

Mental Health Tips

Focus on the moment.	Keep it low key.
Listen to music.	Have an open attitude.
Have a realistic image of yourself.	Stay drug free.
Take everything with a grain of salt.	DON'T try to please everybody.
Keep perspective.	Have applause in your head.
Prioritize and organize.	Do your preparation ahead of time.
Try to do your best.	Take time for yourself.
Get plenty of sleep and take naps when you can.	Have pep talks with yourself and with positive people.

HOW TO KEEP GOOD MENTAL HEALTH:

"I tell myself that this is not the end of the world if I am not chosen. The auditioners are looking for something very special and it may not be what I have to offer."

U of MN First Semester Masters, MA Voice Performance

"Know what helps you feel confident, the tricks that help you feel grounded and full of energy. Not giving the audition too much weight in the grand scheme of things helps me feel prepared to have fun and relax."

U of MN Senior, Theatre Arts

"Prayer, emotional involvement with music."

U of MN Junior, Vocal Performance

"I take care of myself. I'm taking full advantage of these "selfish years," always trying to do what's best for me, being surrounded by family and friends who love me and believe in my talent."

U of MN Senior, Theatre Performance

"I realize that this is a God given gift and it was given to me to make others happy."

U of MN Senior, Theatre Arts

"I try to eat well and exercise regularly when I am not dancing. When I do not take care of myself, my self-esteem and energy are seriously affected. I also try and look nice. When you feel you are dressed well it reflects how you carry yourself."

U of MN Senior, Theatre Arts

"I need to take time for myself and try not to get caught up in everything else that is going on around me."

U of MN Senior, Dance BA

"My teacher just showed me this psychotherapy technique. Lightly tap on your forehead, cheekbones, below your nose, chin, breastbone, palm, and the skin between your thumb and forefinger. Do about ten taps in each area, in that order, with eyes closed. This helps clear your mind of whatever's bothering you."

U of MN Second Year, Vocal Performance

HOW TO KEEP A POSITIVE ATTITUDE:

"Observe life! See theatre, film, dance, and museums. Read plays, books, newspapers. Volunteer at performing venues. Practice cold readings. Continue lessons in music, and get new monologues. Keep a file on auditions."

Barbara Kingsley
Adjunct Faculty
U of MN Department of Theatre Arts

"Do the work you want to do. If there is a group that pays, don't always gravitate to them. Consider working with artists, collaborating to create new and interesting work."

Luverne Seifert
Head of BA Performance
U of MN Department of Theatre Arts

"Don't take anything personally. Audition for everything that's appropriate to one's goals. Network, be in the know."

Maria Cheng
Associate Professor
U of MN Department of Theatre Arts & Dance

"Be internally motivated. Know yourself. Know what stirs your soul. If you don't love your art, get out of it. Believe that you have something to say."

Dawn Baker
Musician/Lecturer
U of MN Department of Theatre Arts & Dance

"Treat each audition as a learning experience, come prepared. You will always leave with something positive."

John Gamoke
Actor/Affiliate Faculty
U of MN Department of Theatre Arts

"My personal approach to this is paradoxical. On the one hand I try to hold myself to a higher standard than those around me. On the other hand I try to not give a damn. You strive always to do the best possible job but you have to be able to laugh off the inevitable failures along the way."

Drew Gordon
Musician in Residence
U of MN

"Enjoy everything you do. Make your career and life in the arts an open road trip instead of a long trip on a super highway to a destination that may be unreachable and out of your control. When not performing dance, sing and see other work. Immerse yourself in an artistic way of life."

Joe Chvala
Artistic Director
The Flying Foot Forum

"Take time away from the theatre when you can! Develop a variety of interests, activities and friends. Use 'down time' to read and research areas you would like to explore in the future. Don't take yourself or your performance too seriously. Do it as well as you can, then let it go. Don't make it your god!"

David Walsh
Director of Opera
U of MN

"Surround yourself with good, positive friends that have a life inside *and* outside the theatre. It is easy to sink into the same attitudes of other out of work actors that like to complain. Develop strong interests outside of theatre like tennis, church, et cetera to bring you back to earth. Don't take it personally if you don't get a job. Forget it and forge ahead."

Linda Talcott Lee
Adjunct Faculty
U of MN Dance Program (Jazz and Musical Theatre)

"Surround yourself with open minded, positive people. Avoid negativity, period. It will get you nowhere fast. Accept praise with humility, knowing there are many talented people out there and no one is indispensable. Learn to take rejection graciously, knowing there are many reasons for it. Stay focused, there's always another show."

Zoe Sealy
Former Head of Jazz Dance Program
U of MN Department of Theatre Arts & Dance

"Realize that it is rarely about you, but rather a different vision on the part of the director. Continue reading new plays and find more and greater roles that you would be right to play."

Shirley Venard
Teaching Specialist
U of MN Department of Theatre Arts

"Constantly work to improve your talents."

Elizabeth Nash
Associate Professor
U of MN Department of Theatre Arts & Dance

Vocal & Physical Health

Drink Lots of Water All Day Long

Increase water intake an hour before you are going to be vocal. Eight to ten cups a day is what's typically recommended. I say have water available at all times so you can drink whenever you are thirsty.

Putting slices of lemon or cucumber in your water makes it taste fresh and gives it a little added flavor.

Limit Caffeine & Alcohol
They tend to dehydrate you.

Avoid Blood Thinners & Antihistamines
Things like Aspirin, allergy medicines, and decongestants tend to dry you out. Try using a nasal rinse to clear your sinuses instead.

Don't Smoke
Limit hanging out in smoky places.

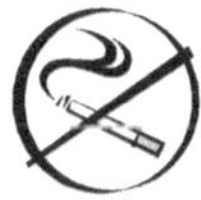

Use Adequate Breath Support
Don't scream and yell too much to prevent straining your voice.

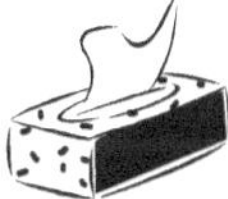

Prevent Sickness
Wash your hands frequently and don't share drinking containers with others. Get enough vitamin C and plenty of rest.

"For the voice: fresh ginger (chopped and boiled, then strained) mixed with honey and lemon."

U of MN Junior, IDIM

Cold & Throat Care Tips

Increase your amount of sleep, fluids, and Vitamin C.
DON'T talk unless you have to.
Try swallowing or drinking water if you have to clear your throat. Coughing irritates your throat further.
Have lozenges *without* a numbing effect if you need to be vocal. Save the numbing products for bedtime.
Use a humidifier while you sleep.
Drink tea with lemon and honey to cut down on mucus. Pineapple juice also works well.
Try caffeine free tea with lemon and Echinacea.
Have something salty like a pickle or gargle with salt water.
Eat an apple to sooth a scratchy throat.
Eating a popsicle soothes the throat and can provide extra Vitamin C.

Eat A Well-Balanced Diet & Treat Yourself Right
Include all of the food groups in your diet to provide yourself with adequate energy. Eat when you are hungry and stop when you are full. When you feel like snacking, try drinking a large glass of water first. Many times we think we are hungry when we are really thirsty. Everyone has something they like to indulge in, so allow yourself a craving once in awhile, but watch the portions. When you treat yourself, enjoy it. This keeps you from over-eating a bunch of other things in order to fill a particular craving.

I keep a bag of extra dark chocolate chips in my refrigerator and grab a small handful when I have a chocolate craving.

Daily Training

Vocal Log
Keep a log of how your voice feels and is acting on a regular basis to determine how your particular instrument reacts to certain foods and stresses. Some people can have a milkshake or yogurt before they sing, while others find that dairy products coat their throat. I find staying away from dairy a couple hours before being vocal helps me. Also, spicy foods are particularly effective in opening up my throat.

Read Out Loud
This is a great daily habit to get into. Reading out loud at least five minutes a day is a great way to practice being articulate and reading new material with energy and ease. Reading out loud can be beneficial for helping with cold readings and for doing voice-over work (which is anytime you hear a voice but can't see the person, such as in radio). It doesn't matter what you read, just try reading clearly and with different dynamics. Practice using different ranges in your voice and adding dialects or character voices. Record yourself and listen to how you sound.

Exercise Regularly
Exercise with about five minutes of moderate movement to warm-up, and at least 20-25 minutes of intense movement for a good cardiovascular workout. Don't forget to take three to five minutes to cool down and another ten minutes or so to stretch. Instead of reading while you workout, which I think slows you down, try listening to inspiring music. Keep your workouts fun and vary what you do. Joining a health club or working out with friends is also a great way to stay motivated. Try to push yourself with a challenging workout at least three to four times a week.

To prevent dehydration, drink a couple of glasses of water before you workout, and more when you are done.

HOW TO STAY IN TOP PHYSICAL & VOCAL SHAPE:

"On top of dancing and singing regularly, I do a (3-4 times a week) regular workout that includes 20 minutes of aerobic activity (high intensity) and a Pilates-style body workout 15-20 minutes/sit-ups, push-ups and floor barre. This has kept me going."

Joe Chvala
Artistic Director
The Flying Foot Forum

"Be honest with yourself. Your body is your instrument. Proper nutrition and exercise is essential to longevity in the business. Continue to hone your skills in order to stay in the best possible performing shape. Becoming stagnant is not an option."

Zoe Sealy
Former Head of Jazz Dance Program
U of MN Department of Theatre Arts & Dance

"You have to train regularly to be an athlete or at least stay in shape. The same goes for an actor. Body, mind, spirit."

John Gamoke
Actor, Affiliate Faculty
U of MN Department of Theatre Arts

"Use the gym, take tai chi, anything that keeps the body active."

Luverne Seifert
Head of BA Performance
U of MN Department of Theatre Arts

Doing Pilates has helped me tremendously. I started by watching a DVD series and now have a twenty minute workout memorized. I do it on a regular basis and have seen great results.

"I like to work daily in a disciplined way as far as maintaining the physical skills. I never miss a day, even if I can only find ten minutes for about eleven months a year. Then twice a year I completely blow things off for two weeks."

Drew Gordon
Musician in Residence
U of MN

"Work out! Do yoga! Take massage!"

David Walsh
Director of Opera
U of MN

"Maintain a healthy diet and physical as well as vocal regimen."

Elizabeth Nash
Associate Professor
U of MN Department of Theatre Arts & Dance

"Warm ups, vocal and body. Get rest and avoid stress as much as possible."

Shirley Venard
Teaching Specialist
U of MN Department of Theatre Arts

For Centering & Balance:	**Yoga, Pilates, Meditation**
For Strength:	**Push-Ups, Sit-Ups, Weight Lifting**
For Flexibility:	**Stretching when you're warm**

Vocal Warm-Ups

It is extremely important to warm your voice up before voice lessons, auditions, rehearsals, performances, or any other time that you want your voice to sound and feel its best. Regular practice of warm-ups will help keep your voice in shape and will allow you to become familiar with what your specific instrument requires on any given day.

Try to do at least fifteen minutes of vocalizing prior to whatever you are warming up for. Some days you may need more, so make sure to leave yourself enough time to do so.

Developing an order of warm-ups that you are comfortable with allows you to do it efficiently. If you're in a hurry, you will not have to think too much about what to do next. Repeat a basic order from day-to-day so you can compare how your voice is doing fairly quickly. This will help if you need to add a specific warm-up to accommodate your voice that day. Do the same set of warm-ups you do on a regular basis before an audition. Make sure to give yourself some time to rest your voice right before an audition. Twenty minutes is usually sufficient.

Singing musical theatre is quite different from singing in a choir. Be able to fully hold your own as a soloist. Be brave, and learn to make loud noises and be unashamed of them. It's okay to make ugly sounds when warming up. The only way to get a nice focused sound is to get through the warm-up. Take chances and keep at it.

The following is a collection of warm-ups that I like to do. The order gets somewhat looser as the list progresses, however, my favorite thing to start out with are lip buzzes.

Lip Buzzes

Put your lips together and blow air through them so that your lips vibrate back and forth. This requires a lot of breath support and gets your breath flowing. It can be done with or without a piano. If your nose starts to itch a little, then you are doing it right.

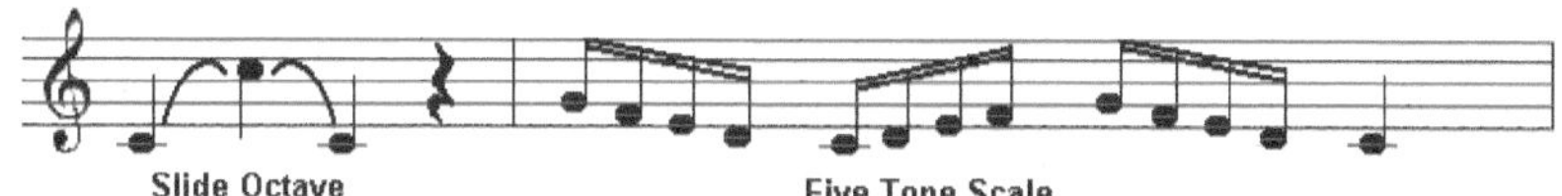

Panting

Ninety seconds to three minutes of panting can help to increase your breath capacity. If you do this one often, over time you will notice a greater ability to sustain your breath for longer periods of time. (This one is easy to do during any free time you have throughout the day).

Facial Massage

Loosen your tongue by massaging underneath the chin with a thumb while relaxing your tongue inside your mouth. Relax your jaw muscles by massaging your face where the bottom and top teeth meet while applying a gentle pressure. Move your tongue around the inside of your mouth and lips to stretch out your cheeks.

Tongue Trills

This one took me about six months to learn. Some people can naturally trill their tongue, but it can also be learned. The technique is used to help roll "r" sounds, such as those used in Spanish. It also helps loosen your tongue. Similar to the lip buzzes, you need to use a lot of breath support to do this. If you can't do it at first, practice moving your tongue as fast as you can on a "la." Eventually, you will be able to get it.

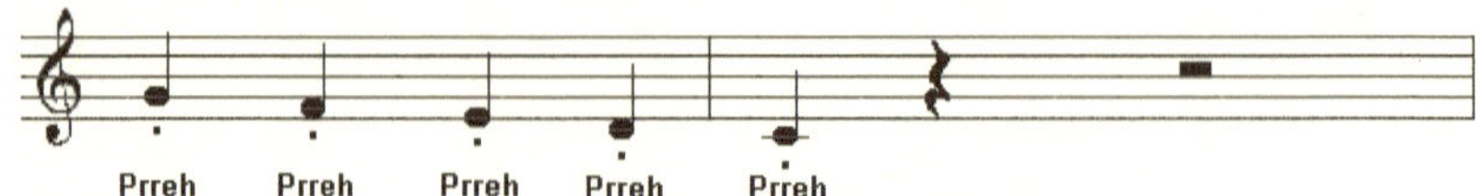

Humming

Hum any number of things, including your songs or simply a tune on the radio as you drive to your rehearsal or audition. This helps gently get your vocal chords moving before you actually start singing.

Vocalizing

Try to gently warm your voice up by working the middle vocal range first. Then, stretch your range to reach your lowest and highest range. Practice singing legato (slow and sustained) and staccato (quick and light). Go by how it feels, rather than how it sounds. How we hear ourselves is quite different than how other people hear us. The goal is to get a nice core sound with a strong breath support.

Middle Voice

For this one, feel a ring behind the nose.

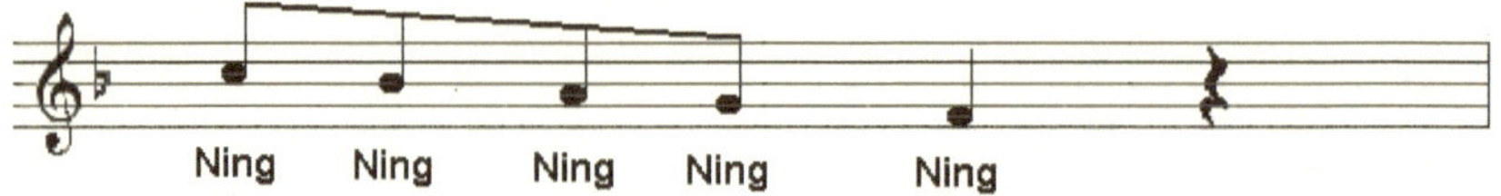

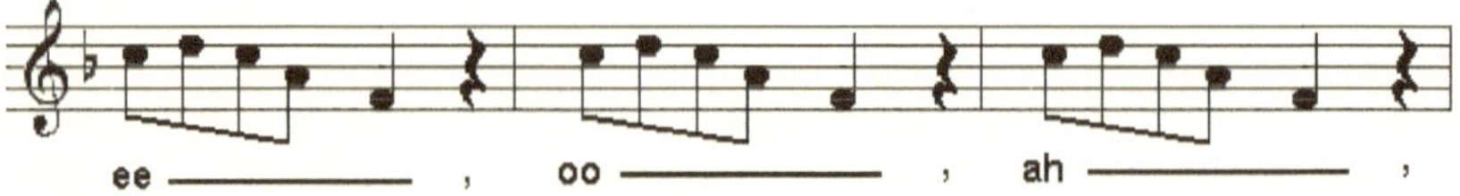

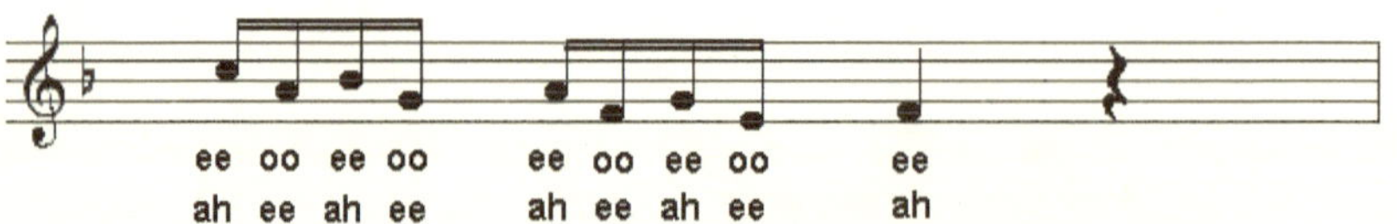

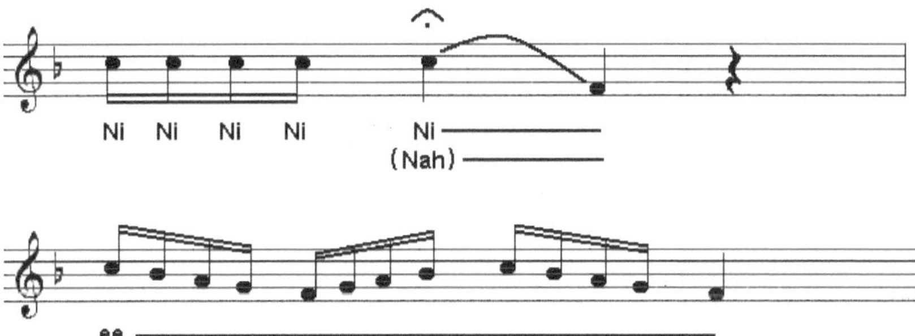

Lower Voice

Do this quickly, moving down by half steps.

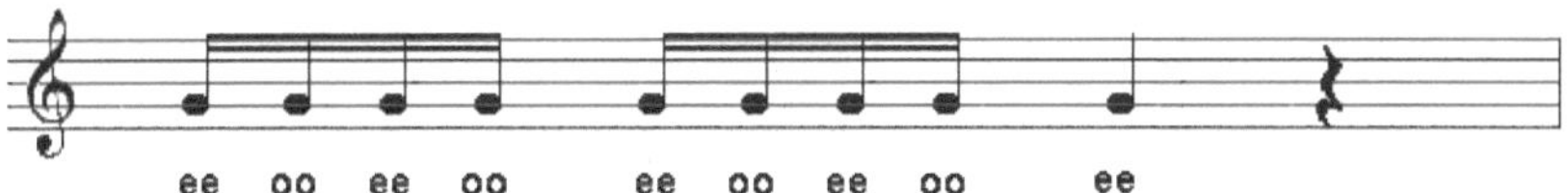

This one can be helpful to loosen the tongue as well.

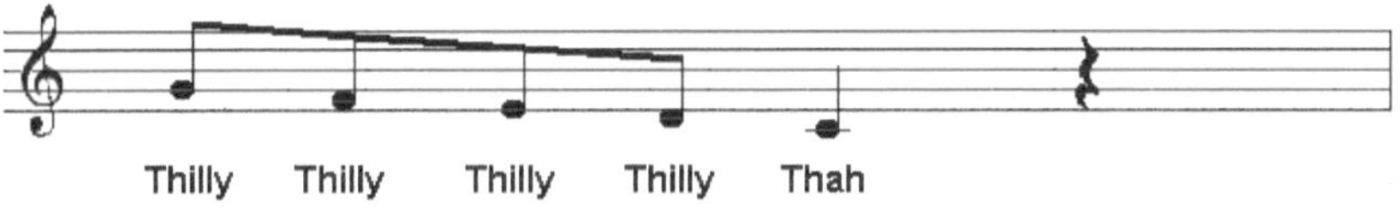

Upper Voice

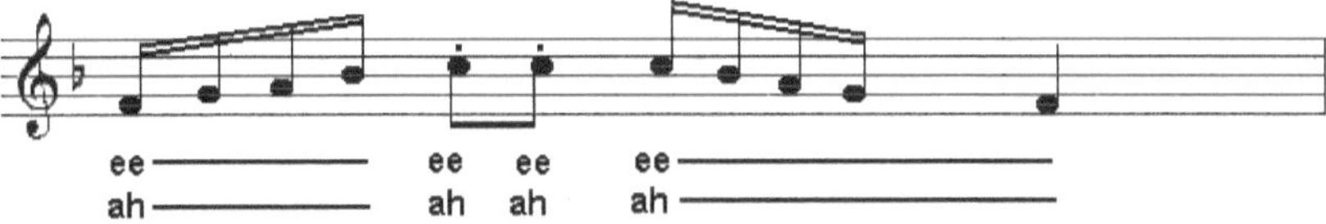

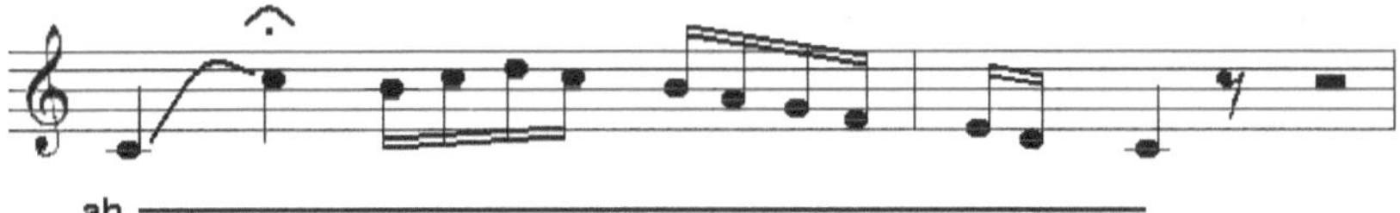

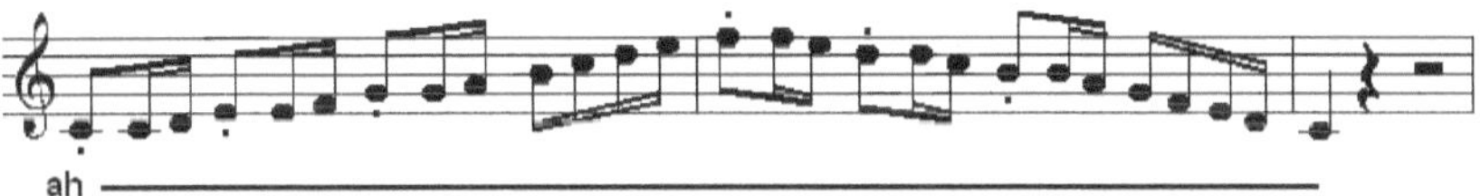

Do this slowly, with consistent breath.

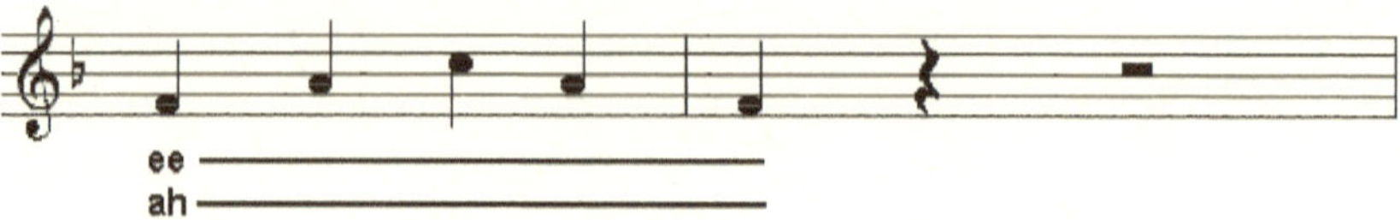

This one is good for diction as well.

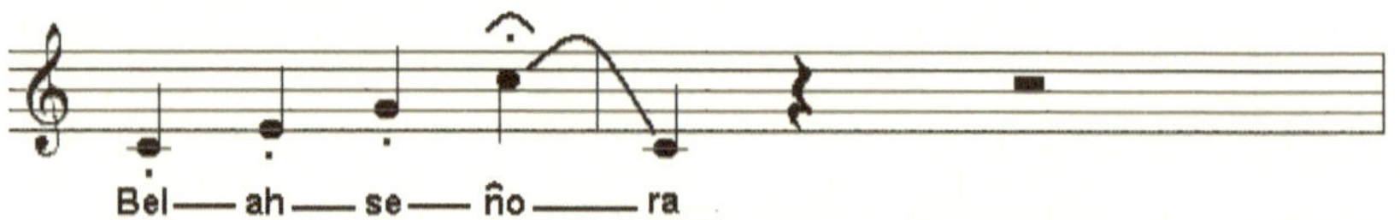

Focusing Nasal Voice, Head Voice, & Chest Voice

Try singing with different focuses. Focus the sound forward into your nasal cavities, upward into your head, or downward into your chest. Careful not to press or force your voice where ever you are focusing it. Play around with moving it back and forth and feel the differences between each area.

This one is good for diction as well.

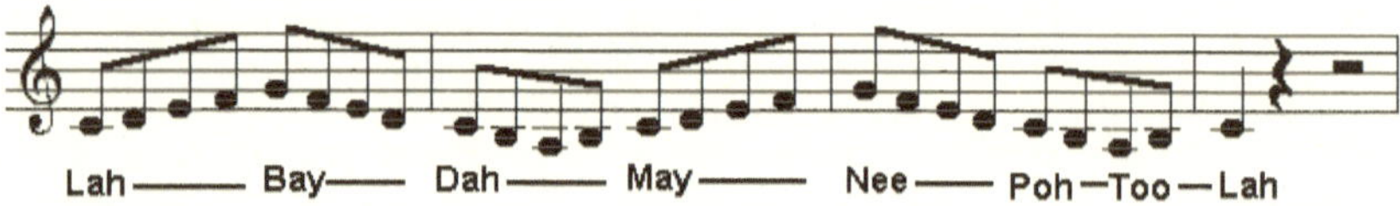

Counting

Counting from one to eight and back down from eight to one on scales is a great way to get your mind connected while you are singing. Start with 1, and then add another number each time while always going up a half step to the new number and back down the scale to 1.

1...1,2,1...1,2,3,2,1...1,2,3,4,3,2,1... et cetera.

This can also be reversed if you start with 8 and go down a half step to the new number each time while always going back up the scale to 8.

8...8,7,8...8,7,6,7,8...et cetera.

Increase your speed for a greater challenge. Visualize that you are going up and down stairs as you move from number to number.

Tongue Twisters

There are any number of fun ways to get your mind and mouth connected. You will often need to add a few new phrases to your warm-up so that they stay challenging. These help with diction and wake up your mind as well.

This specific one works well with: Aluminum Linoleum Aluminum & Toy Boat, Toy Boat...

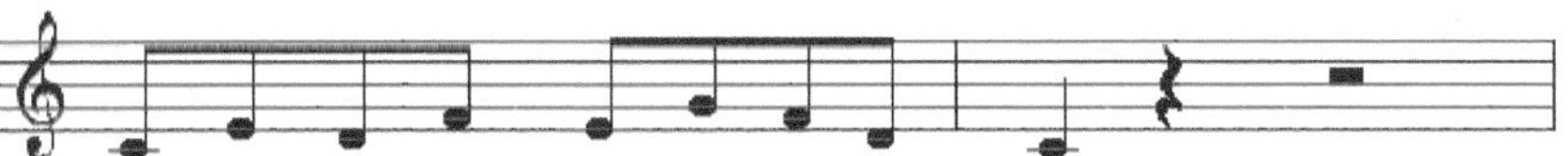

Some other ones to try:

- Unique New York, Unique New York, Unique New York.
- Red Leather, Yellow Leather, Blue Leather.
- A Big Black Bug Bit A Big Black Bear, Made The Big Black Bear Bleed Blood.
- Who Washed Washington's White Woolen Underwear When Washington's Washer Women Went West?
- A Cup of Proper Coffee In A Copper Coffee Cup.
- Sheep Shouldn't Sleep In A Shed. Sheep Should Sleep In A Shack.

Sirens

Make loud siren sounds starting very high in your register and dropping to very low in your register. Make sure to use good breath support, and try to make the transitions seamless. It's great for projection and connecting your registers.

Additional Warm Ups

Finding Range & Key Signature

At first this may seem a bit confusing, but don't worry it takes some time to grasp.

Finding Range

Just find the lowest and highest note in the song. Make sure you can reach each note. This will be one of the first things you will want to look at when picking out a new piece to perform for auditions.

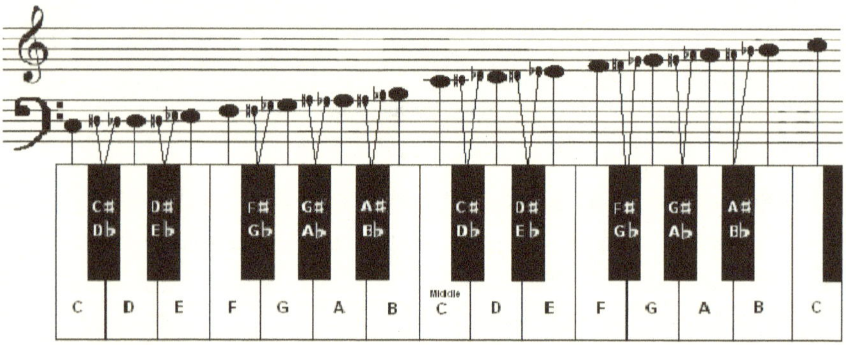

Key Signatures

Located at the beginning of your piece of music, the key signature is useful to look at so you know if the music is easily playable. Try to avoid songs with five or more sharps or flats. Look at the diagrams provided to better understand key signatures. Together the flat and sharp key signatures form a circle, which musicians refer to as "The Circle of Fifths." Each key is a fifth or seven half steps apart. The minor keys are a third or just three half steps below the corresponding major keys.

Flats

Look at what note the second to last flat is on, except when there is one flat: Then it is F Major. The order of flats is: B, E, A, D, G, C, F. To remember this, use the mnemonic device: "Before Eating A Doughnut Get Coffee First."

Sharps

Look at the last sharp and go one letter beyond that alphabetically. The note that the last sharp is on is what's called the "Leading Tone." This means it is one note below the "Tonic," or what the key signature is. So, if the last sharp is on D the key signature is E Major. The order of sharps is: F, C, G, D, A, E, B. (The exact opposite order of the flats) To remember this, use the mnemonic device: "Fat Cats Go Down Allies Eating Bugs."

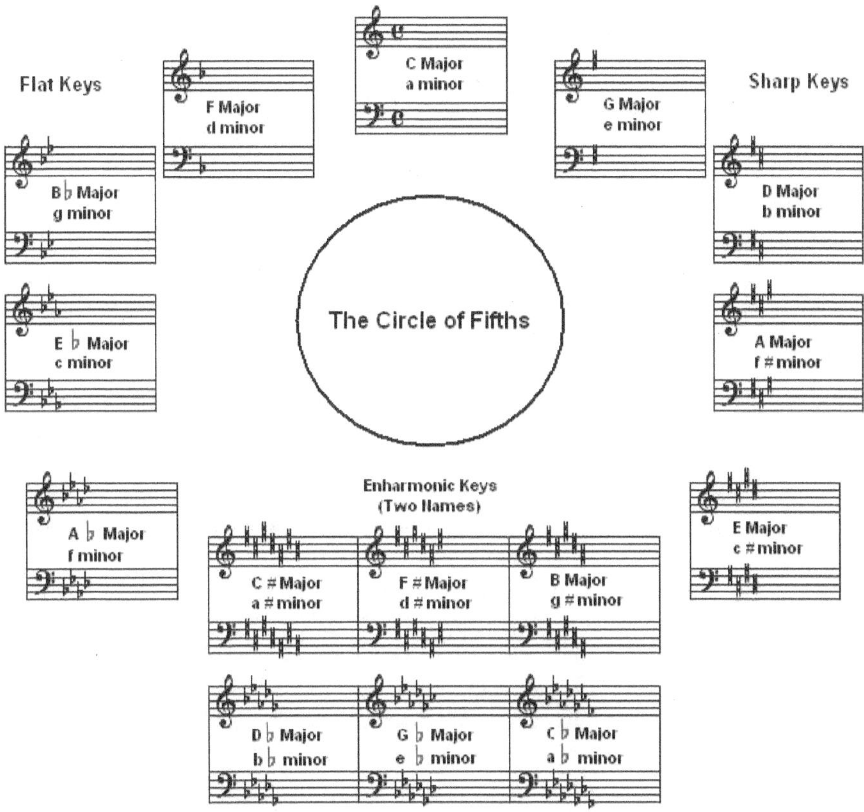
Flat Keys
F Major
d minor
C Major
a minor
G Major
e minor
Sharp Keys
B♭ Major
g minor
D Major
b minor
The Circle of Fifths
E ♭ Major
c minor
A Major
f # minor
A ♭ Major
f minor
Enharmonic Keys
(Two Names)
E Major
c # minor
C # Major
a # minor
F # Major
d # minor
B Major
g # minor
D ♭ Major
b ♭ minor
G ♭ Major
e ♭ minor
C ♭ Major
a ♭ minor

Physical Warm-Ups

Before doing any physical stretches you need to be warm enough so that your muscles can relax. Doing things like running in place and jumping up and down, can quickly get your blood flowing and your body temperature rising.

It is beneficial to physically warm-up and stretch before doing any physical or vocal work, so that you prevent injury and prepare your body for what you will be asking it to do.

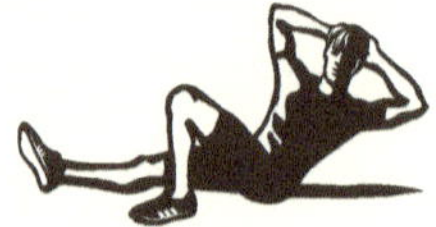

Face & Eyes

- Open your eyes as wide as you can while lifting your eyebrows and opening your mouth in as big of a face as you can make. Reverse, and squeeze your eyes as tight as you can while pulling your lips together to make the smallest face possible.
- Open your eyes wide. Look up, down, and to the sides with as much focus as possible.

Head, Neck, & Shoulders

- Roll your head around in a circle while being careful not to crunch the back of your neck when your head tilts backwards. Repeat circles to the other side.
- Roll your shoulders forward in a circle while allowing them to lift up towards your ears and then push them down away from your ears. Repeat circles backward.
- Push your shoulders up to your ears with tension and drop them to relax.

Spine & Torso

- With feet shoulder width apart, stretch to the side with both hands clasped over your head while supporting your abdominal muscles. Reverse to the other side.
- With the same grasped hands, allow the stretch to drop down to the floor as you bend at the waist and make a large circle. (You can add lip buzzes with this one.)
- Rotate your upper torso with your arms out to your sides. Allow your head and focus to go with you as you move back and forth.
- Bend forward and drop your arms and hands to your feet. While supporting your abdominal muscles, allow your head and neck to relax and for gravity to gently pull you closer to the floor. Shake your head yes and no for added stretch to your neck and head.

Full Body

- Do what is called the "Downward Dog" in yoga, or the "Inverted-V" stretch on the floor. With your feet and hands shoulder width apart, bend over and walk your hands out in front of you on the floor. Press your heals gently to the floor, while you press through your shoulders and hands as your rear end forms the point of the V-shape. Support your abdominal muscles and feel a stretch through your entire body.

- Lie on the floor and rock your body back and forth with your heels moving slightly. Every so often, stop and rest as you let your body sink into the floor. Feel your breath rise and fall to release tension.
- Lie on a tennis ball and move it around while gently applying pressure. Continue breathing and allow for your body to relax into the pressure points you are creating. (You can also apply pressure to your feet. Roll the ball under your arches while standing.)

Unions

If you are pursuing performance as a career, you should consider becoming a member of a union eventually. Unions offer benefits for performers like healthcare, pension, and emergency relief funds. They also set restrictions on the number of hours you can work and give you contract protection. If problems arise, they will represent you as a professional. There are also some scholarships available for students.

Actors Equity Association (AEA) www.actorsequity.org
Actors Equity Association is a nationally recognized union for professional stage actors. There are three types of contracts: Principals, Chorus, and Stage Managers.

The number of Equity theaters will vary from state to state. In Minnesota there are currently twenty-one Equity theaters including: *The Guthrie, The Children's Theatre*, and *The Chanhassen Dinner Theatres.* However, they also hold auditions for Non-Union performers as well. If you end up being cast in one of their shows, you may be eligible to become a member of the union if you choose. Some theaters will require you to become a member. There are also *Small Professional Theaters* (SPTs) that cannot afford to hire all Equity, so they hire both Union and Non-Union performers.

To become a member of AEA, you will either have to sign an Equity contract, or you can become an *Equity Membership Candidate* (EMC). EMC requires you to pay $100 up front and for you to work fifty weeks in Union houses. The weeks do not have to be consecutive and there is no time limit on how long it takes you to complete. Check the AEA website for the current initiation fee and yearly dues.
If you join you will receive what is called an Equity Card, which says you are an official member of AEA. These cards change often and you will get a new one at least once a year.

To receive benefits you have to work twelve weeks to get six months coverage. After twenty weeks of work you can receive a year's worth of coverage.

Screen Actors Guild (SAG) www.sag.com
Screen Actors Guild is a union for professional actors in television and film.

American Federation of Television & Radio Artists (AFTRA) www.aftra.com
American Federation of Television & Radio Artists is a union for professional actors in television and radio.

There is a lot of crossover between SAG and AFTRA. There has even been talk about merging the two unions. They offer similar benefits as AEA and are also recognized nationally. Large companies such as *Target* and *Best Buy,* based in Minneapolis, provide many opportunities for work in commercials and radio. Check for similar companies in your area.

To become a member of SAG or AFTRA you need to be hired under one of their contracts. Check the SAG and AFTRA websites for the current fees to join and yearly dues. Payment plans are available.

American Guild of Musical Artists (AGMA) www.musicalartists.org
American Guild of Musical Artists is a union for professional opera performers and dancers.

Does being Union have an impact on the amount of work you may get? What are the advantages & disadvantages of being Non-Union?

"Being in a Union definitely has an impact on whether or not you are hired. In NYC, for a Broadway Show, you have a better chance of being hired if you are AEA. Equity members are allowed to audition first, with Non-Equity seen if time allows. Conversely, there is more work for Non-Union members in NYC and across the nation. Many of the "First National" tours are going Non-AEA, taking a lot of work away from Union members. In all cities except NYC, the Union contracts are very limited."

Linda Talcott Lee
Adjunct Faculty
U of MN Dance Program (Jazz and Musical Theatre)

"Yes, once you've gotten past getting your foot in the door, and have acquired a credible amount of experience. Advantages are: One has fewer restrictions when seeking work. There are many venues for Non-Equity performers today to gain experience and build a resume. For performers with limited experience just starting out it is to their advantage to be Non-Equity. Disadvantages are: No benefits and unable to draw unemployment. Non-Equity salary is also smaller as a rule."

Zoe Sealy
Former Head of Jazz Dance Program
U of MN Department of Theatre Arts & Dance

"In Minneapolis there is often a strange balancing act of Equity versus Non-Equity where either position can be of benefit. Generally the rule is the category with lots of people (young women in their 20's) is generally cast as Non-Equity and the rare category (old men) is cast as Equity. There are Equity quotas beyond that hiring Non-Equity is more economically feasible. NYC is a different story. Equity cards save you time getting auditions and you always get paid better if you are Equity."

Joe Chvala
Artistic Director
The Flying Foot Forum

Agents, Managers, Casting Directors

These are people who can help you market yourself and find you jobs if you decide to pursue performance as a career. Although you can get work without one of them, your chances may be better because they often have connections you do not.

Having a manager in California or New York is much more common than having a manager in Minnesota. However, there are plenty of agents and casting directors in the Twin Cities area. Look in the telephone book under "Talent Agencies" and "Casting Directors" for contact information. You can also check online to find what's available in your area.

Getting an agent and being seen by casting directors takes some work. Start by sending out your headshot and resume to the local agencies and casting directors. Include a short cover letter that says something like: "May I take this opportunity to introduce myself...I have studied at...performed in...would like to be considered for representation, et cetera." A cover letter will give a reason to separate you from a pile of other headshots and resumes.
Make sure to include references that you have prior approval to use and highlight who recommends you. If you get permission, include your references' e-mail addresses or phone numbers.

Being persistent is key. After you have auditioned for someone, mailing a short-hand written thank you letter is appropriate. Whenever you are in a show, mail a show postcard with your headshot to the agencies and casting directors to let them know you will be performing. Invite them to come, and offer a complimentary ticket if you have one. The key is to get your face and name recognized as much as possible.

In New York, performers often set up what is called a "Meet & Greet." This is not an audition, but a chance to be seen and talk to agents and casting directors during a five minute interview. If you plan on going to New York and are interested in finding an agent or being seen by casting directors, send out your headshot, resume, and a letter that tells when you will be in New York. Be unique. Tell them what you have recently been in and that you would like to set up a "Meet & Greet."

Agents

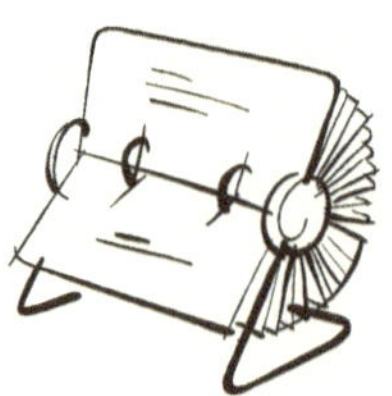

- Have to be licensed by the state.
- Will suggest the best way to market you.
- Work to find you jobs.
- Have access to "Breakdowns," or private listings for types directors are looking for.
- DON'T charge you for service unless you get hired.
- Negotiate a contract for you.
- Usually get 10-15% of your pay when you are hired.
- *Association of Talent Agents* (ATA) www.agentassociation.com

Shop around for an agent. Ask around to see who people recommend. Have some questions ready, such as, how many clients they have and how often they see their clients' work.

If you plan on doing any work under an AFTRA contract make sure the agent is a "Franchised Agent." This means that they have entered into an agreement with AFTRA regarding contracts and following certain rules. If you are asked to sign a contract with an agent, make sure you understand everything first. When you are just starting out, you may want more than one agency working for you.

If you sign with an agent be patient. It can take quite a bit of time to get work. Sometimes they just may not have anything for you. It also takes time for your face and name to get known. But remember that they are working for you.

Managers

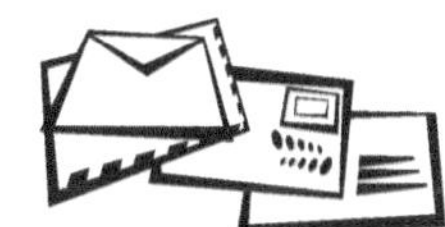

- DON'T have to be licensed by the state.
- Will suggest the best way to market you.
- Work to find you jobs and guide your overall career.
- Find you work through personal connections.
- DON'T have access to "Breakdowns."
- Can charge you for service before you get hired.
- DON'T negotiate contracts.
- Can charge 15% of your pay when you are hired.
- *Talent Managers Association* (TMA) www.talentmanagers.org

Casting Directors

- DON'T have to be licensed by the state.
- Will find you work because of the way you market yourself.
- Hired by theatre companies and directors to find talent for them.
- *Casting Society of America* (CSA) www.castingsociety.com

The Ross Reports

The *Ross Reports* is a monthly trade paper that has all of the current agents, managers, and casting directors in New York. Because shows open and close so quickly, the agents and casting directors change often.

Networking

It is extremely important to build a network with people in the business. Keep track of people you have worked with and directors you would like to work with. Take note of their e-mail address and phone number if they have given it to you. Stay informed about what they are all currently doing. Write down when you have seen their work or have read something about what projects they are currently working on. This will be helpful information to remember the next time you speak with them, because it shows that you care and have an interest in their work. If you show your interest, you are making a connection that may help you in the future. You never know, some day you may be auditioning for a friend or colleague from college or a previous production.

Put the names in an address book or on index cards in a file box especially for contacts. The key is to have it organized so that you can easily keep track of the information you need. Categorize it by Directors, Choreographers, Cast Members, Teachers, et cetera.

You may also want to consider joining an online networking tool such as facebook.com, which allows you to stay connected with your contacts, as well as make new ones.

Today, e-mail is such a great way to instantly make contact with people. Sending out an update to all your performing friends every few months can be a great way to keep in touch once you are out of school. Do this shamelessly. Let people know what you are up to by sharing successes and troubles. It is more than likely they will be able to relate to you. It may take some work, but it is definitely worth having friends and keeping them.

The Day Job

If you plan on having a career in performing, you will most likely need a second job. Since most theatre takes place at night, having a day job is probably the best choice. Despite what most people think, waiting tables is not the only option you have. Although it can be a great way to make fast cash, there are plenty of other routes to take.

If you are Non-Union and need health insurance, keep that in mind when you are looking for a job. Look for a job that is flexible enough that you can take off for an audition. Ask the employer ahead of time whether they will work around your schedule.

The job should not be completely draining or cause a lot of stress. This type of job will vary from person to person, but whatever you choose make sure it feeds you with positive energy. Remember, if you have a job you hate you will have nothing left to give to your performance career.

Think about other aspects of the performing arts business that interest you. Working for a box office or finding an agency to hire you as a receptionist are great ways to still do something within the business. Teaching is an option as well, depending on how much experience you have.

Other options may include doing commercials, print work, voice-overs, or industrials. (Industrials are things like corporate training videos that are typically not seen by the general public.) These usually have very good pay, and normally require only a few hours of work. This type of work is another way to hone your creative talents and get your name and face out there.

If you have other interests or hobbies, see if someone will hire you in that area. Working in a field completely separate from your performing career may provide a nice diversion.

Taxes

This section may be a bit overwhelming at first, but in the end you can save yourself a lot of money. If you plan on making a living performing, it is crucial that you keep track of your money very carefully. The goal is to pay the least amount of tax that you are legally responsible for. The key to reaching that goal is to keep excellent records of where you are getting your money and what you are spending it on.

There are two ways that you will most likely be making your money as a performer. The first way is as an employee, and the second is as an Independent Contractor.

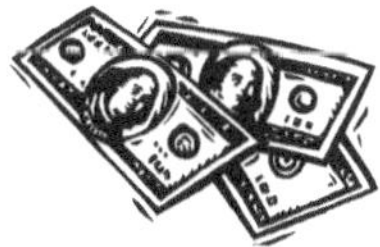

Employee Work

- Union members can only be paid as an employee.
- Get check with withholdings for Federal, State, Social Security, & Medicare.
- Will record all income on a 1040 tax form or W4.
- Will record all non-reimbursed employee expenses on a "Schedule A" 2106 form.

Independent Contractor Work

- Is like running your own business.
- Get lump-sum check with no withholdings, which means you owe tax.
- Will record all income on a 1099 tax form. (An employer is only obligated to send you a 1099 if the total amount for the year is $600.00 or higher.)
- You owe a "self-employment" tax which covers what you would have paid in Social Security and Medicare, and what your employer would have owed for Federal and State. (This comes out to roughly forty cents to the dollar) You may want to take out 40% of the check, if you can afford it, and put it away so that you will have the money you owe when it comes time to pay up.
- "Schedule C" section on a tax form is used to record all non-employee business expenses. It helps you reduce taxable non-employee income by taking all of your untaxed income and subtracting your expenses. For instance, if you made $20,000 you could easily have $15,000 of work expenses. Which would leave only $5,000 of taxable non-employee income.) A HUGE SAVINGS!! When first starting out, it is not impossible to have more expenses than what you actually made that year.

The IRS requires a business to show a profit three years out of every five or they can declare your business a hobby. After such a determination, they will only allow you to reduce your income to zero.

Keeping Good Records

This is necessary in case you are audited by the Internal Revenue Service (IRS). An audit is an examination of your tax return, and may be triggered for various reasons. The best way to avoid an audit is to assume the IRS knows nothing about your business. You should provide them with as much information as you possibly can. Penalties for false information may result in fines for tax fraud. You should keep your records on file for at least seven years before shredding them.

Keep records by using

- Financial Software
- The Old Fashion Spreadsheet
- Date Books

Things you need to record

- Any income you make as a performer or elsewhere. (Save check stubs).
- Employee and Independent Contractor expenses you require to run your business.

Deductible Expenses

These are anything that you can prove are needed in order to run your business. You are not required to keep receipts for anything under $75 as long as you keep a record of it in a timely manner. A canceled check alone is not a receipt. A canceled check with a receipt is better than just the receipt itself, but the IRS does not accept a canceled check as sole evidence of a deductible expense. (You *do* have to keep ticket stubs for shows and receipts for "meal and entertainment," see below.) You should note whether each is an Employee or an Independent Contractor expense.

Self Promotional/Marketing Materials

- Headshots
- Resumes
- Audio Recordings, Video Reels
- Postcards/Announcements
- Websites and other expenses for giving yourself a presence on the internet
- Trade Advertisements
- Agency Talent Books
- Agency Commissions (ALWAYS on union jobs, on non-union jobs only if YOU pay them, not if the agency takes their cut before paying you.)

Supplies

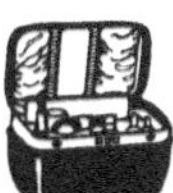

- Stage Makeup
- Wardrobe Expenses
  The IRS rule for deducting clothing is this: If you can wear it on the street, you can't deduct it. Exceptions are made for formalwear (tuxedoes and dress gowns.) Otherwise the item has to be a legitimate COSTUME. So, if you buy a glitter-covered suit for your cabaret act, THAT'S a costume and is deductible. If you buy an Armani suit for auditions or even to wear in a show, that is considered street wear and is not deductible.

Cell Phone (ONLY if you have another primary/home phone)
- You will be required to give a percentage of how much it is used for business purposes.

Internet Access (ONLY if you can prove you need it to find work, et cetera.)
- You will be required to give a percentage of how much you use it for business purposes.

Tickets to Shows
- Theatre and Movies are considered research for your business. (You must save your ticket stubs.)
- Tickets to see YOU for agents, directors and casting folk.

Piano Tuning/Moving/Equipment Repair

Art Supplies
- Fabric, notions, scissor sharpening

Trade Papers
- Friday & Sunday New York Times, Sunday Star Tribune in Minneapolis has job listings

Backstage Tips to Dressers (NO GIFTS, checks only!)

Car and Truck *Gas Mileage* (NOT deductible for mileage to a primary job.)
- To auditions/interviews
- To a temporary job from home, if you have a primary job
- To a temporary job from your primary job
- To an unpaid performing job (It is advertisement when agents and other possible future employers come to see you.)
- Keep track by using your trip odometer.

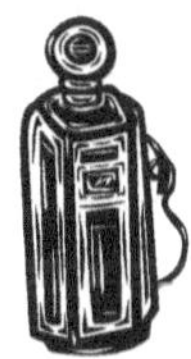

Meal and Entertainment for business purposes.

- You must save the receipt. (The expense will be halved to subtract your share of food.)
- You must supply the date, place, name of person you met and their title or function, and what you talked about.
- Check the standard daily meal allowance for the city or state you're in.

Business Travel

For each trip, be sure to note: how many days you were traveling, if you were working or looking for work, the start and end date (or anticipated end date), salary or compensation, per diem (if any), or extras (i.e., room provided).

- Airfare to auditions out of state
- Hotel expense for the day of the audition
- Local transportation in travel location: auto rental, bus, subway, taxi
- Travel to and from airport (bus, cab, limo)
- Local phone expenses for business
- Laundry/dry cleaning

Qualified Performing Artist

Since all EMPLOYEE BUSINESS EXPENSES (as opposed to non-employee Schedule C expenses) are a miscellaneous deduction, most young actors who take the STANDARD DEDUCTION don't qualify for them. The IRS has provided a narrow work-around for extremely impoverished actors to take a portion of their employee expenses as a straight ADJUSTMENT TO INCOME rather than a miscellaneous deduction. A "qualified performing artist" is an actor or other performing artist who:

1. Performed services in the performing arts as an employee for at least two different employers during the tax year.
2. Received at least $200 each from two employers.
3. Has expenses attributable to the performing arts which add up to 10% or more of their gross income from the performing arts.
4. Had an adjusted gross income of $16,000 or less before deducting expenses as a performing artist. If the performing artist is married they must file jointly with their spouse.

See the instructions for IRS Form 2106 for more information.

Whether you hire someone to do your taxes or you do it yourself, it has to be done. You may use the free VITA tax program offered through AEA and SAG in the major cities (New York, Los Angeles, et cetera). Internet tax programs such as "Turbo Tax" can also be very helpful because it will catch errors and prompt you as you go. You should keep a hard copy if you go this route. If you decide to hire a "Paid Preparer," you should assume they know little about your business. Many do not understand what a person in a performing career can deduct, this is why *you* must.

FINAL THOUGHTS

"Be serious about your craft but don't take yourself too seriously. Be ready and flexible. Be clean, on time and sober."

Drew Gordon
Musician in Residence
U of MN

"If you have a passion to do this work, it will dictate all your choices. If you lose the passion-act accordingly. If you don't lose the passion you will also act accordingly but not, perhaps, what your family considers "accordingly."

Luverne Seifert
Head of BA Performance
U of MN Department of Theatre Arts

"Do what you love but know how to do office work or have some other skill so you don't have to work for people that you don't feel right about. Don't sell your soul or yourself."

Dawn Baker
Musician/Lecturer
U of MN Department of Theatre Arts & Dance

"Be yourself-stay focused and persistent in your pursuit of work. Listen to others, but most of all your inner voice when making career choices. Be generous in your support of others, which in turn will reap many benefits for you, not only in your chosen profession, but throughout your life in general."

Zoe Sealy
Former Head of Jazz Dance Program
U of MN Department of Theatre Arts & Dance

"Fear is false evidence appearing real. The way out of fear is giving."
"There are no impossibilities only possibilities."
"Don't think too much. If you get it, you get it."
"Keep your own council and try to answer questions yourself."

Shirley Venard
Teaching Specialist
U of MN Department of Theatre Arts

"I could not have imagined my life as it is now at age twenty. Being open to changes in my course and ready to jump through the open doors instead of trying to beat down the closed ones has made my life in the theater richer than I could have ever imagined."

Joe Chvala
Artistic Director
The Flying Foot Forum

APPENDIX

Additional Resources

Sheet Music and Vocal Scores

Groth Music Store www.grothmusic.com
Schmitt Music Store www.schmittmusic.com
T.I.S. Music Catalog www.tismusic.com

Plays, Monologues, Musical Scores, and Cast Recordings

Samuel French Bookshop www.samuelfrench.com
The Drama Book Shop www.dramabookshop.com

Regional Theatre Opportunities

Regional Theatre Directory
Updated each year, this book has a listing of all the productions that will be produced in the United States according to each region. It also lists where and when each show will be holding auditions.
Summer Theatre Directory
Similar to the *Regional Theatre Directory*, it lists all the productions that will be produced in the summer months. It also lists where and when each show will hold auditions.

Tax Information

The New Tax Guide for Performers, Writers, Directors, Designers and Other Show Biz Folk: From How to Get Organized to What to do if You Are Audited, including a Monthly Expense Diary
By R. Brendan Hanlon, ISBN-13: 9780879102760

Trade Publications & Magazines

American Theatre Magazine
This magazine has information on various theatre related topics.
Hollywood Reporter www.hollywoodreporter.com
This focuses on Hollywood business.
The Back Stage West, previously known as Drama-Logue
Similar to New York's *Back Stage*, this trade paper is written in Los Angeles.
Variety www.variety.com
This is a weekly trade paper from New York with stage, theatre, & film news.
Variety Daily
Written in Los Angeles, it is the West coast version of *Variety*.
Village Voice www.villagevoice.com
This is another trade paper written in New York.

Tickets, Broadway and Hollywood News

Broadway.Com www.broadway.com
This has ticket information, hotel packages, an online gift store, and Broadway news.

Internet Movie Database www.imdb.com
This is great for looking up the credits for your favorite film and television performers.

Internet Broadway Database www.ibdb.com
This is great for looking up the credits for your favorite Broadway stars.

Playbill Online www.playbill.com
This has reviews, links to other theatre websites, and access to purchasing discounted tickets.

Other Helpful Websites

Minnesota Association of Community Theatres www.mact.net
This website has audition notices for community theatres in Minnesota.

Minnesota Film & TV Board www.mnfilmandtv.org
This website has production guides, information on talent agencies, and a hotline that is updated weekly regarding the need for movie extras in Minnesota.

Minnesota Playlist www.minnesotaplaylist.com
This website lists auditions for the Twin Cities area and you can either search or set up a profile on the talent list they provide.

Minnesota Talent Website www.mntalent.com
This is a great resource for free online resume and headshot space, or to get information about on-camera work, agencies, and classes.

Midwest Theatre Auditions (MWTA)
www.webster.edu/depts/finearts/theatre/mwta
Each region in the United States has what are called Regional Theatre Auditions, which are auditions that are held for a combination of around sixty companies and theaters in the region. It can be a great way to be seen by a large number of people at once.

Spring Board for the Arts www.springboardforthearts.org
This has an online resource handbook specifically for Minnesota Artists.

SWE Sound Productions, Inc. www.swesound.com
This is a website with links to local theaters in Minnesota.

Theater Communications Group (TCG) www.tcg.org
This is the website for the National Organization for American Theatre.

The Dramatists Guild of America www.dramaguild.com
This website includes information on playwrights, composers, and lyricists.

Suggested Readings

Aaron, Stephen. *Stage Fright: Its Role In Acting.* Chicago, IL: University of Chicago Press, 1988. A good one for any performer to read.

Bering, Rudiger. *Musicals: An Illustrated Historical Overview.* New York: Barron's Educational Series, Inc., 1998. This talks about the evolution of musical theatre in a historical context.

Botto, Louis. *At This Theatre:100 Years of Broadway Shows, Stories and Stars.* New York: Applause, 2002. A great coffee table book with lots of pictures and stories, it talks about each Broadway Theatre in New York and the shows that have been produced in each of them.

Cameron, Julia. *The Artist's Way: A Spiritual Path to Higher Creativity.* New York: Penguin Puttnam Inc., 2002. This was highly recommended by a former voice teacher to help find inner creativity.

Cohen, Robert. *Acting Professionally: Raw Facts About Careers In Acting (Sixth Edition).* New York: McGraw-Hill, 2004. This book is just awesome!

Craig, David. On *Performing: A Handbook for Actors, Singers, & Dancers on the Musical Stage.* New York: McGraw-Hill, 1987. Check out this handbook as well.

Gottfried, Martin. *All His Jazz: The Life and Death of Bob Fosse.* New York: Bantam Books, 1990. A biography about the influential choreographer and director of musicals, Bob Fosse.

Green, Stanley, and Kay. *Broadway Musicals: Show by Show (Fifth Edition).* Milwaukee: Hal Leonard Corp.,1996. A brief synopsis of each musical including names of original cast members, choreographers and directors.

Hagen, Uta. *A Challenge for the Actor.* New York: Macmillan Publishing Company, 1991. A great book by the German actress and teacher who lived in my home town Madison, Wisconsin.

Jowitt, Deborah. *Jerome Robbins: His Life, His Theatre, His Dance.* New York: Simon & Schuster Trade, 2004. A biography of Jerome Robbins, another very influential musical theatre choreographer.

Kislan, Richard. *The Musical: A Look at the American Musical Theater.* Englewood Cliffs, NJ: Prentice-Hall, 1980. This covers the basic principles and evolution of the American Musical.

Maslon, Laurence. *Broadway: The American Musical.* Little, 2004. A companion book to the terrific PBS *Broadway Series,* this takes you through the history of the American musical.

Shurtleff, Michael. *Audition: Everything an Actor Needs to Know to Get the Part.* New York: Walker, 1978. A how-to book that unlocks the mystery of Auditioning.

Silver, Fred. *Auditioning for the Musical Theatre.* New York: New Market Press, 1985. Another recommended book that includes tips on auditioning specifically for musical theatre.

Stevens, Gary, and Alan George. *The Longest Line: Broadway's Most Singular Sensation: A Chorus Line.* New York: Applause, 1995. This one includes interviews, photographs, and memorabilia from one of the longest running shows on Broadway, "A Chorus Line."

WORKS CITED

1 Cohen, Robert. *Acting Professionally: Raw Facts About Careers In Acting (Sixth Edition).* New York: McGraw-Hill, 2004.

2 Stephens, Kent. "Monologues: Before and After." University of Minnesota Acting Course Handout. 2001.

3 Sealy, Zoe. "Dance Auditions: Do's and Don'ts." University of Minnesota Musical Theatre Course Handout. 2004.

4 Baker, Dawn. "Accompanists and Auditions." University of Minnesota Musical Theatre Course Handout. 2004.

5 Baker, Dawn. "Accompanists and Auditions." University of Minnesota Musical Theatre Course Handout. 2004.

6 Sealy, Zoe. "Dance Auditions: Do's and Don'ts." University of Minnesota Musical Theatre Course Handout. 2004.

7 Mann, Paula. "Stages of the Creative Process." Lecture in Dance Improvisation, University of Minnesota, 9 Dec. 2003.

8 Stephens, Kent. "Character Advocacy, or You Gotta Love 'Em." University of Minnesota Acting Course Handout. 2001.

9 Stephens, Kent. "Behavior: What Is It?" University of Minnesota Acting Course Handout. 2001.

10 Stephens, Kent. "The Ten Big Questions, Revised." University of Minnesota Acting Course Handout. 2001. Based on Uta Hagen's ideas in: *A Challenge for the Actor.* New York, Scribner, 1991.

I consulted with a local Twin Cities Tax expert for the information about taxes. They wish to remain anonymous.

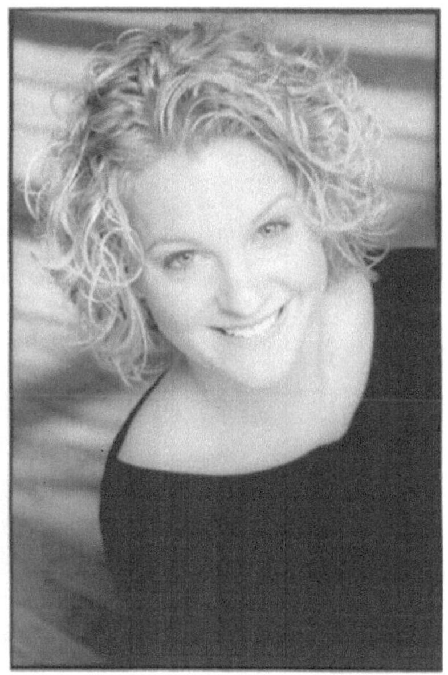

ABOUT THE AUTHOR

Originally from Madison, Wisconsin, Andrea Uselman moved to the Twin Cities in the fall of 2000 to study in a rich theatrical community while attending the University of Minnesota. She designed her own Music Theatre Major through the College of Liberal Arts' Department of Individualized Degrees. Her areas of study included courses in music, theatre, and dance. Uselman graduated from the University of Minnesota in December of 2004. *Beyond Talent* was inspired by her senior project and desire to help performers reach their goals. She is currently pursuing a performance career in the Twin Cities and living with her husband Tim.

www.ingramcontent.com/pod-product-compliance
Lightning Source LLC
LaVergne TN
LVHW050941080826
845145LV00004B/1351

* 9 7 8 0 5 7 8 0 0 3 2 8 3 *